D0362669

PRACTICAL IDEALISTS

Changing the World and Getting Paid

PRACTICAL IDEALISTS

CHANGING THE WORLD AND GETTING PAID

ALISSA S. WILSON
ANN BARHAM
JOHN HAMMOCK

PUBLISHED BY
GLOBAL EQUITY INITIATIVE
HARVARD UNIVERSITY

DISTRIBUTED BY HARVARD UNIVERSITY PRESS
CAMBRIDGE, MASSACHUSETTS 2008

Copyright 2008. Alissa Wilson, Ann Barham, and John Hammock.
All rights reserved.
Published 2008.
Printed in the United States of America.

Library of Congress Cataloging-in-Publication Data

Wilson, Alissa S., 1978-
Practical idealists : changing the world and getting paid / Alissa S. Wilson, Ann Barham, John Hammock.
p. cm.
ISBN-13: 978-0-674-03207-1
1. Social service--Vocational guidance. 2. Career development. 3. Social action--Case studies. I. Barham, Ann. II. Hammock, John, 1944- III. Title.
HD8039.N65W55 2008
361.7'63023--dc22

2008011157

Cover Design by Jill Feron/Feron Design.
Layout by Oona Patrick.

This book is dedicated to Tina Hammock, Karen Marguerite Wilson, and Pat and Jerry Barham.

Contents

Acknowledgements

We are humbled by the people who make up this book. We have always known that practical idealists are everywhere, but it was an honor to hear firsthand so many stories of inspiring work. We are forever grateful to those who shared their stories with us and, through us, with you. They serve as reminders of what individuals can accomplish alone and together.

The idea for *Practical Idealists: Changing the World and Getting Paid* first came from John's wife, Tina, who thought John should write down his experiences working at international nonprofit agencies and raising a family. She believed that it could serve as an example to young practical idealists who were also trying to do social change work. The need for practical idealist models was also reinforced time and again in John's ethics class at the Fletcher School of Law and Diplomacy at Tufts University. His graduate students all wanted the perfect partner and the perfect job that would allow them to change the world, and, of course, make enough money to live reasonably well in our society. In response, John joined forces with one of those students, Alissa Wilson, who had studied voluntary action for the public good as a Jane Addams–Andrew Carnegie Fellow at the Center on Philanthropy at Indiana University. The Practical Idealism Project and this book were under way.

At about the same time, John began work on another project that would also shape this book. He joined with Dr. Sabina Alkire to set up an initiative that would challenge current economic thinking. Based on the pioneering work of Nobel Laureate and economist Amartya Sen and others, Sabina and John believed that to successfully and sustainably reduce poverty it was essential to change the way poverty was perceived and measured.

Economists (and others) needed to broaden their narrow focus on income and growth as the indicators of development or poverty reduction, because income was just one of a series of dimensions essential for well-being. Sabina and John agreed that what was needed was an effort that would not only undertake first-rate foundational research but also translate the findings of that research into policy. The Oxford Poverty and Human Development Initiative (OPHI) was launched in 2007 at Oxford University to fill this need.

It is the authors' belief that just as OPHI is challenging conventional economic models, the practical idealists in this book challenge traditional thinking as to what is possible for individuals within our current society. They, too, are interested in income and growth, but they are equally committed to living out their values and to a broader concept of their well-being. These practical idealists are fully extending their personal capabilities to further their personal development. Human development at the personal level is the essence of practical idealism and the subject of this book.

The headquarters for all of us throughout this work was the Global Equity Initiative (GEI) of Harvard University. This center at Harvard seeks to advance the understanding and tackle the challenges of equitable global development. Global inequity—both among people and nations—is among the greatest challenges of our times. Severe disparities exist not only in wealth, but in health, education, economic opportunity, democratic freedoms, and access to new technologies. Despite the urgency and importance of these issues, our understanding of the forces and consequences of severe inequity is critically limited. Even less clear is the path to a fairer and more just world. GEI brings together scholars, policymakers, and practitioners from around the world to address these problems.

One of the programs at GEI focused on the role of philanthropy in meeting the challenges of inequality. Through this program, GEI sought to advance the understanding of global philanthropy and to strengthen the role of private philanthropic investments in advancing global equity. Scholars at GEI investigated corporate, foundation, and individual charitable giving. Practical idealism, by contrast, turns this program on its head. Instead of characterizing philanthropy as giving financial resources to help others, practical idealism is giving one's own time and talents towards the building of a more equitable world founded on the well-being of everyone. Philanthropy thus defined is not just about giving money or assets; it is about living out the meaning of one's own life for the benefit of others through modeling practical idealist behaviors and involvement in social change.

We thank GEI for its support of this project. We are particularly grateful to Erin Judge who helped once the writing was done and the manuscript had to be turned into a book. We also thank Oona Patrick for her excellent layout and copyediting skills.

The Practical Idealism Project would not have been possible without the generous support of Ursula and Robert Jaeger. We thank them for their faith in our work, their continuous encouragement, and their commitment to human development.

The chapter on finances would have been far less detailed were it not for the timely assistance of Ana Hammock Isen, assistant director of financial literacy at ACCION USA. Ana shared her expertise regarding financial literacy and provided much of the information on credit card debt.

This book would never have made it into print without the gracious help and vigorous backing of our friends and colleagues at Tufts University. For two years this project was supported by the Jonathan M. Tisch College of Citizenship and Public Service at Tufts, where John was awarded a fellowship to work on practical idealism. The financial and administrative staff at the Fletcher School, particularly Karen Mollung, has been invaluable and instrumental. We are indebted as well to the Gerald J. and Dorothy R. Freidman School of Nutrition Science and Policy for their support, especially Patricia King.

We end by once again thanking the practical idealists from around the country who took time out of their active schedules to speak to us. Our interviews and descriptions are mere snapshots of their dynamic and vigorous lives. Indeed, as you'll learn in the biography section, many have already moved on to new challenges and opportunities. We are also grateful to friends and colleagues who gave us enthusiastic encouragement as well as great suggestions about whom to interview. These practical idealists represent only a fraction of a much larger community. Their actions and choices show us that we can all live our lives in ways that acknowledge that both our well-being and the well-being of others matter.

1. Choices Matter

The Practical Idealism Project was officially born in November 2005 when Dr. John Hammock and Alissa Wilson began gathering the stories of practical idealists, or people who express their values and passions through their career and life choices. John had been teaching at Tufts University for twelve years. He had come to Tufts after nearly three decades of international development work. His career included directing Oxfam America for eleven years and ACCION International for seven years. As a professor at Tuft's Fletcher School of Law and Diplomacy, he often talked to students who told him about their own desire to work for social change at an organization like Oxfam. Their hopes, however, were usually accompanied by anxiety about paying student loans, achieving financial stability, and having enough time for families and personal lives. Alissa was one of those students. She was studying conflict resolution and political analysis and had come to Fletcher after working in the United States and Nigeria. As graduation approached, she too had student loans to pay along with a dedication to social change.

While John had many years of experience working as a practical idealist and balancing a family with a career, Alissa was just starting out. She had many questions about how to build a career, have a positive impact on society, and balance financial and personal responsibilities. Though they represented nearly opposite ends of the life experience spectrum, they shared a commitment to practical idealism. Alissa and John knew from their conversations with students and friends that many people wanted to be practical idealists. They just didn't know where to begin and lacked examples that could help them. *Practical Idealists: Changing the World and Getting Paid* was written with those friends and seekers in mind. If you are on the path of practical idealism, then this book was written for you too.

In this book, John and Alissa draw on interviews with over forty practical idealists, as well as on their own experiences, to illustrate how you can succeed as a practical idealist. The practical idealists in this book are international development workers, lawyers, business people, artists, social workers, computer techs, union researchers, activists, stay-at-home parents, health outreach workers, and city managers, just to name a few. They are all working to transform society and getting paid to do it. These are not trust fund beneficiaries. They paid rent, bought houses, paid off student loans, had families, and made comfortable lives for themselves. They knew that the naysayers who had told them that they could not work for social change and survive financially were wrong. They include people like the following:

- *Samantha Yu, Director of Policy Analysis, Los Angeles Commission for Children, Youth and Their Families.* Samantha studied political science in college and enjoyed it so much she was thinking about a PhD in the subject. An internship in the LA mayor's office led her to change her plans and pursue a Masters of Public Policy. She now works to ensure that the city's services for children are coordinated and effective.
- *Josh Dorfman, Founder and CEO, Vivavi, New York.* As an explorer of the many things life has to offer, Josh has been a ski bum, English teacher in China, factory manager, MBA graduate, screenwriter, and PhD student. In the end, he found a job that brought together all his interests and experiences. He created a design firm to help people understand that their houses could be both stylish and environmentally responsible.
- *Torrey Dixon, Fellow, University of North Carolina Center for Civil Rights, Chapel Hill.* Torrey graduated from the University of North Carolina's School of Law. After graduation, he committed himself to supporting rural minority communities in their fight for basic rights from the state.

- *Kelly Letzler, Executive Manager, Just 'Cause Catering, Indianapolis.* What do you do when your great loves are food and social work and you have a culinary degree? Kelly manages a catering company that supports its parent organization Second Helpings. Second Helpings runs food rescue, hunger relief, and job training programs.
- *Araceli Simeón-Luna, National Parent School Partnership Director, Mexican American Legal Defense Fund, Los Angeles.* Araceli's father wanted her to study computer programming, a degree he thought would guarantee her a job that paid well. Instead, she took her parents' appreciation of education and made it her career. Araceli became the director of the Mexican American Legal Defense Fund's National Parent School Partnership program.
- *Jennifer Jordan, Research Analyst, Service Employees International Union, Washington, DC.* Jennifer supports workers in salary and benefit negotiations. She uses her investigative talents and number skills to research and run the numbers on the finances of the hospitals with whom they are negotiating.

The Practical Idealism Project demonstrated that practical idealists can have any type of educational background and work in the private, public, or nonprofit sectors. They can also self-identify in any number of ways, including Type A or Type B personality, traditional, or nonconformist. A practical idealist might be an MBA who wouldn't touch a pair of Birkenstocks, or a hemp-wearing environmentalist. In organizations throughout the country, these are the people who have asked themselves questions about how they can have a life that they enjoy, make an impact on society, and still pay the bills. The practical idealists John and Alissa interviewed are only a sample of the thousands of people who opt for social change careers that reflect their values.

Practical idealists:

- see a connection between their individual choices and social change;
- take time to evaluate their actions and choices in light of their value system;

- are not content to merely envision positive change but are committed to making choices in their own lives that will help them bring that change about; and
- are well informed about their options.

They have all confronted the questions that you may be currently facing:

- Can I be an idealist in today's world?
- Can I make enough to live reasonably well and also live out my values and my idealistic dreams?
- Can I have meaning in my life through my work, my relationships, and my free time?

Their answer (and Alissa and John's) was a resounding "Yes!"

In reading the stories of practical idealists, you will become familiar with the many possibilities and challenges of practical idealism. It is not always easy, but it is doable. *Practical Idealists: Changing the World and Getting Paid* is intended to encourage and inspire, as well as provide concrete tools for making the kinds of choices and decisions necessary for the practical idealist life. Through examples and exercises, the book explores how you can:

- clarify your values and passions;
- learn relevant skills;
- find work;
- understand money issues and personal finance;
- create supportive community; and
- use college and graduate school effectively.

These chapters were constructed to respond to the questions asked most frequently by people on the path of practical idealism. They reflect the lessons John and Alissa learned from the Practical Idealism Project and through their own experiences. More information, including additional transcripts of interviews with practical idealists, is available at the project website: www.practicalidealists.org. After reading about the lives of practical idealists and carefully considering the questions posed, it will be apparent that you too can live in a high-speed, modern society *and* respect your values while enjoying a balanced life.

PRACTICAL IDEALISM & REFLECTION

> So I got in my car, drove to Montana and went to a pawnshop, bought a fishing rod, a guitar, and a "guitar for dummies" book, because I actually don't play the guitar. And [I also bought] a case of beer and checked into a motel and was like, "All right, the plan is about to go into action."
>
> —Josh Dorfman, Founder and CEO of Vivavi

> Ideally, I believe, you make it [the decision about your future] best by really brainstorming with other people and going through a very intentional process about what is important for you. And if I could really do anything differently, it would've been to be more intentional, earlier on in my past.
>
> —Chris Estes, Executive Director,
> North Carolina Housing Coalition

Chris Estes took part in a vocational retreat sponsored by a group called Stone Circles in North Carolina. Josh Dorfman drank microbrews and learned the chords for "House of the Rising Sun." Clearly, people set out to make important life decisions in many different ways. You don't have to drive out for a solitary visit to Missoula or go on a special retreat to figure out "what's next" on your practical idealist path. You can do it anywhere—a coffee shop, your living room, the park....The crucial actions are to stop and think—to develop a steady habit of reflection. Practical idealism calls for thought, contemplation, and, at times, patience. It is a commitment to personal transformation tied to a vision of social, political, and economic change. This can only be done if you take the time to know yourself, to understand your own values, passions, and needs, and allow yourself to be guided by this knowledge.

Such reflection is not a one-off occurrence. Practical idealists continually check in and compare the reality of their lives with their values and passions. Some of our practical idealists meditate and a few pray, while many just set aside "quiet time." Still others participate in formal discernment exercises in a structured group setting. This chapter will get you started on your own reflection process by asking you to think about your values, your passions, and "how much is enough?"

Passions and Values

> Here I am with a social service agency, but I'm cooking and doing what I love! It's a good blend of everything.
>
> —Kelly Letzler, Executive Manager, Just 'Cause Catering, Indianapolis

Kelly Letzler is passionate about food as well as the importance of helping people gain skills and achieve self-reliance. Kelly's current job with Just 'Cause Catering, a revenue-generating project for a food rescue, job-training, and hunger relief organization, lets her fulfill these two passions. Allison Greenwood Bajracharya, another practical idealist, works for the Los Angeles Unified School District and is committed to education issues. As a young teacher with Teach For America in New Orleans, she had students who had never owned a book. Confronted with the staggering inequities and institutionalized racism of that educational system, she reports that "education definitely became my issue—and my passion."

Like Kelly and Allison, all of the practical idealists John and Alissa interviewed could articulate a specific passion or group of passions—an idea, a community, a kind of work—that informed their career choices. These practical idealists had also taken the time to examine their core values and then placed these values at the center of their professional and personal lives. In every case, they had come to their work because it corresponded to their passions and values.

The interplay between your passions and your values will be the foundation for your practical idealism. For example, if you hold economic fairness as a value and are passionate about the environment, you might work for good air quality in economically disadvantaged regions. On the other hand, if you are excited by politics and its processes, you might work for equity by lobbying local governments to provide low-income housing for their citizens or work in government to enact legislation for school improvement. Thinking seriously about your values and your passions allows you to shape the form your practical idealism will take.

Take some time to read and answer the two questions below. Write down what first comes to your mind and then consider whether that is genuinely what you believe at your core. Spend time answering these questions even if you think you know exactly what you want to do to express your practical idealism. Doing this exercise can only serve to solidify what you have already established. The practical idealists we spoke with took the time to check in with themselves about what they were doing; these types of questions allow you to do that.

Questions:

1. What are your values? What do you believe in? Many people initially find it challenging to put their values into words. Often the first difficulty is getting a clear idea of what, exactly, *values* means. *Values* can be a vague term that people avoid because it has been used by some groups to criticize or marginalize other groups. For the purposes of this question and this book, however, values are simply the conclusions you've reached by thinking about what you've experienced or believe to be true. Values are the ideas that bring order to people's ethical lives. At times your values may originate with experience and reasoning and at other times your values may emerge from faith or an inner sense that something is right or wrong. A value might be, for example, the idea that all people were born equal and possess certain inherent and inalienable rights. It could also be a judgment about how people should treat one another or the conviction that your overall life's goal should be to lessen suffering wherever you find it.

   Once you have made your list, make a note of which of these principles you could not, under any circumstances, compromise. Which values are worth more than your own personal security?
2. What are your passions? What gets you up in the morning? (If you have been sleeping in a lot lately, what *would* make you bounce out of bed—besides the promise of a really excellent donut?) Are you motivated by a deeply felt connection to others? Are you guided by religious faith? What about art, creativity, or political philosophy?

> Passions are not always noble or grand but they are powerful. Are you driven by the conviction that a good education should be accessible to all people or that no child should die of a preventable disease? Are you compelled to ensure that you will never be without material comforts? Are you motivated by the desire to lead or impelled to succeed in order to prove naysayers wrong? Are these passions long-standing or have they emerged more recently?

Don't be anxious if your list of passions and values seems incongruent or too unfocused. This is not uncommon. You may have come across the old Greek adage, "The fox knows many things, but the hedgehog knows one great thing." Some people, in other words, range over a greater territory of passions, while others burrow into one central passion that informs all their other choices. It may seem that the single-passion hedgehogs will necessarily have an easier time figuring out the desired path of their practical idealism. But foxes can also find ways to integrate their diverse passions with their practical idealism. Remember Kelly Letzler? She was able to successfully marry her passions for food and social work. Kelly is not the only one; practical idealists manage this feat all the time.

If you're feeling stymied while answering these questions, consider what you might have said when you were younger. What would you have answered in high school? Maybe you once had passions and interests that you would have liked to have pursued, but you were told to choose something more "practical." Exploring passions that you had at an earlier age might help to clarify some of the things that are still important to you now—even if you haven't thought about them in a while.

After answering these questions, take one more look. Are there things that you don't really want to be on the list? Can you trace the origins of your values and passions? While origins are not everything, understanding why certain things are important to you is part of an effective reflection process. Jennifer Jordan, for example, is a research analyst for the Service Employees International Union who supports workers' salary negotiations. She shared this story about her family: "My parents have had one bumper sticker all of my life. It was a Catholic campaign for human development sticker that read 'If you want peace, work for justice.' It's only been one. It never changed. Never an election bumper sticker, it was just that one."

After you have written down your passions and values, talk over your lists with a trusted friend or friends. Ask them if they agree with your findings. A good friend can be a valuable reality check. This approach is particularly helpful for practical idealists who would rather work things out through conversation and dialogue instead of in quiet self-reflection.

How Much Is Enough?

If the previous section on values and passion tended to focus on the idealism of practical idealism, this next section centers on a practical question: "How much is enough?" Your financial needs and desires will play a large role in your answer to this question. As our practical idealists will vouch, however, "How much is enough?" does not just apply to money. Quaker organizer Noah Merrill, for example, explained that he was so busy with work that his earned vacation days went unused. How much time off do you need? Josh Dorfman declared that running his own eco-friendly furniture and design business was so demanding that he "spent three years married to [his] company." How much time do you need to spend with friends and family? Laura Hogshead spoke about the value of personal fulfillment versus money. What is "enough" success?

Money

Like it or not, one of the thorniest dilemmas facing those who wish to be practical idealists is how to have enough money to live well, but also have a job that allows them to have meaning in life. John often hears students say that they cannot take a practical idealist job and live well. There may be some truth to this; it depends on your definition of living well. It is possible in today's world to live well and do good with a job in education, nonprofits, government, public service, farming, or small-scale businesses. Likewise, practical idealists can be attorneys, physicians, mutual fund managers, or corporate executives—they just need to avoid being sucked into a way of life that precludes mindfulness and doing good for society.

James Forman, Jr., a former public defender and now a professor at Georgetown Law, for example, had this to say:

> I tell my students about how you can actually pay off your debt while having a low paying job. And nobody believes me. But I sit down with them and go over housing expenses; I talk to them about having a roommate; I talk to them about not having a car. We do budgets, and I tell them that the number one thing you have to do to make it is that whenever you get a raise, because even in public defender jobs you do get raises, what you do is you take half of your raise and you add that to your loan repayment and you never see it. You do monthly automatic withdrawals so you never see the money.

Time

As we mentioned earlier, "How much is enough?" is not just about money. The amount of time that you spend at your job will have a large effect on your ability to pursue other interests, cultivate the relationships you have, and create new relationships. Elizabeth Ouzts, state director of Environment North Carolina, spoke about time as one of the aspects of her career that makes it hard to put a life together.

> Choosing this kind of career involves more sacrifices than just money sacrifices, right? The only example that I can think of—and I'm sure that there are more—is that if I worked forty hours a week and had a six-figure salary, I would be miserable for forty hours a week but I would take swing dance lessons at night and go to a pottery class. I would help start a local co-op or something, you know? There are all these things that I value in my life. I still do those things, but definitely not as much as if I didn't have to work so many hours to do my job.

The number of hours that a job takes can eat into your ability to have a life whether or not you are a practical idealist. Time for outside work activities, whether it's swing dancing, spending time with an already established community, or meeting new people, is important. Take a while to think about how much time you need.

Time and money questions:

1. How much, in terms of time and money, is enough for you? At this point, we're not asking you to do a detailed budget, just to answer this question with as much descriptive detail as possible.

   A response might be: Enough money to afford a two-bedroom apartment, prescription drugs, basic cable, retirement savings, flights home twice a year, dinner out twice a week, macchiatos every morning, season tickets to the Red Sox, et cetera. Enough time might be at least three weeks of vacation, minimal travel, and getting home almost every night by seven.
2. Are your wants consistent with the values and passions you listed earlier? What, if anything, do you value more than money or time?

   Laura Hogshead, assistant director of the Center on Poverty, Work, and Opportunity, for example, talked about forms of compensation beyond the financial:

   > Even though you may be choosing something that is paid less handsomely, in terms of life and in terms of happiness, you are rewarded more if you really feel connected to the job you're doing—if you're not frustrated by it every day. It is hard to make that choice, especially when you are looking at financial burdens and keeping up with your friends and going on trips and things like that. But this work is so rewarding that you have to put a value on that too and realize that your sanity and happiness and how you feel about yourself is important too. There isn't a price tag that you can put on it but you have to weigh it in that consideration.

3. Look back at your answer to question number one. Which "wants" really connect with your most deeply held passions?

   Before accepting her current job, Alissa estimated how much it would take to pay rent, feed herself, get around, make student loan payments, and still have fun. Having joined a summer dance program as her first act out of grad school, Alissa was certain her version of "enough" had to include money for dance classes. She knew that whenever she had lived for an extended period without dance, she had been miserable. For some people dance classes would have been a luxury, but for Alissa it was something that fed her spirit and even enabled her to do better work. What is the equivalent of dance for you? New books? Dinners out? Gifts for friends? Travel?

Success and prestige

The role of success and prestige can be another balancing act for practical idealists. Often, the words *success* and *prestige* are used interchangeably, but they do not mean the same things. Prestige or status is decided by external factors; it is bestowed upon you on the basis of a certain title or income or the recognition and regard of others. While success may be characterized in such ways, it can also be measured by internal means—by your own personal definition of achievement.

In his second year out of law school, James Forman, Jr., clerked for Chief Justice Sandra Day O'Connor. The prestige of his position meant that at the end of his clerkship he would be offered a signing bonus of $50,000 to work for a big law firm. Many would say that this path was success—a graduate from Yale Law School, a clerk for a Supreme Court Justice, and an associate for an important law firm. James, however, knew that his definition of success was a little different. He came from a family involved in the civil rights movement and his values reflected that history.

> I really saw the absolute tragedy or travesty that is indigent defense representation at the trial level. The legal representation that people get when they are poor, they are charged with a crime, and they face trial is the biggest scandal of the criminal justice system. Everything else, to me, pales in comparison to the fact that we have so few quality lawyers [as public defenders] and we pay them so little. The results are what we see—a lot of people who don't get due process. So I thought, "Well, I better go and be a public defender. That is what I was complaining about so let me put myself on the front lines and do that."

James Forman, Jr.'s, story is not unusual for a practical idealist, but it is admittedly not the cultural norm. External validations, like salary and prestige, remain common measuring sticks for success. For example, while James's parents may have understood his career choice, when Torrey Dixon graduated from law school he felt that his family was a little disappointed that he was an attorney who did a lot of community organizing and behind-the-scenes work: "They were expecting me to be an attorney that goes to the courthouse every day with my briefcase. They had the traditional idea of what an attorney should be." Nevertheless, Torrey reports, "I think that the meaning that I found in it definitely outweighs all of those things."

Questions:

1. How do you define success? Is it determined by the size of your salary or by your accomplishments? How important are titles, awards, and recognition from your peers?
2. Why do you think this is your understanding of success? Is it the definition that you want it to be?
3. How important are the opinions of others in shaping your assessment of your success?

CHOICES MATTER

An understanding that choices matter and that personal choices are tightly linked with social change is the hallmark of practical idealism. Practical idealists continually reevaluate where they are, where they have been, and where they want to go. They are clear about their own choices and how those choices affect their community and their world.

As you evolve as a practical idealist, it is up to you to take control of your own personal transformation. Practical idealism demands an ongoing discussion with yourself about your values and passions. It also requires you to think about your place within your family, community, and society. This process is not easy. Like social change, effective personal transformation takes time, effort, commitment, and confidence. In the chapters that follow, we will continue to explore how other practical idealists have made their choices. Their stories and examples will act as signposts as you make your way along your own practical idealist path.

2. Skills

In the last chapter, we asked you to reflect on your passions, your values, and how much was enough for you to live a satisfying and meaningful life. Now, we want you to consider the skills that are necessary for the work you plan to do. We particularly want you to consider the skills you already have and how you can develop your abilities in order to accomplish the work you want to do.

While no specific skill set is required to be a practical idealist, it has been our experience that successful practical idealists tend to have certain skills in common. These skills fall into three broad categories: strategic, personal, and organizational. While some of these skills are clearly abilities that can be learned, others may not immediately seem to be "skills" at all but rather core aspects of one's personality. Nevertheless, we believe, and this was confirmed by our interviews, that all of the skills we discuss can be cultivated regardless of your disposition—though your temperament will, in some cases, determine how easily you pick up some of them.

Strategic skills, which allow practical idealists to envision the big picture and to place their lives and work in a broader context, include information gathering and analysis, political action, and ethical awareness. The second set of abilities, personal and behavioral skills, are, not surprisingly, the most temperament-sensitive capacities of the three skill categories. These encompass risk-taking, taking initiative, listening, and remaining open to experiences outside of your comfort zone. The final category of organizational and development skills is the most technical of all the skill sets and helps practical idealists implement strategies for social change. There are, of course, many types of technical skills, but the three organizational and development skills that John and others have found particularly critical are communications, administrative management, and promotion (sales).

STRATEGIC SKILLS

Practical idealists use their strategic skills to understand the world around them and their relationship to that world. Strategic skills include analyzing social problems in the social, political, and economic context in which they take place. Strategic skills also help practical idealists understand the ethical dimensions of the strategies they create and choose. You can develop these skills in many different situations, including during paid work or volunteer work, formal education, and in everyday life with family and friends.

Information Gathering and Ongoing Analysis

The first step in strategic thinking is gathering information and performing an ongoing analysis of your findings. Strategic thinking enables practical idealists to:

- identify complex problems;
- recognize the various forces that affect these problems;
- understand how the forces that affect complex problems are interconnected; and
- create strategies to address the issues that have been identified.

James Forman, Jr.'s, work as a co-founder of the Maya Angelou Public Charter School in Washington, DC, exemplifies the four components of strategic action. When James started out as a public defender in Washington, DC, he often worked with juvenile defendants. He quickly learned that even when a judge or prosecutor agreed that incarceration was not the best option for a young offender, the city lacked alternatives.

> I realized that we had this incredible batch of highly trained, aggressive, committed lawyers all running around the city trying to find the perfect program for kids. The problem was that

> there weren't enough good programs. There were more good lawyers than there were good programs for those good lawyers to find. I thought about that and I asked myself what I could do about it. I started to talk to my clients about "what would work for you?" They didn't want to get locked up, but they also didn't like the options that they had. I started talking to educators as well about what they thought would really work. [As a result] David Domenici and I started an after-school tutoring and job-training program for kids.

The importance of gathering information prior to acting might seem like a "no brainer," but many people, often very well-intentioned, act on preconceived notions and incomplete information. Particularly when your goal is to help an individual or a group of people, basing your plan of action on what *you* think is best, without the input of those affected, is a dangerous arrogance. James could have taken his Ivy League education and started a program that *he* thought his clients needed. Fortunately, he took the time to gather essential information. James spoke to his clients about what they thought would work for *them* and asked experienced educators to weigh in as well.

> [Co-founder] David [Dominici], who was a lawyer at a law firm at that time, bought this little tiny pizza shop on the corner of Florida and North Capital. We incorporated this little nonprofit and we had six kids. They were clients from the public defender's office. The deal was, they wanted to work and they wanted to get paid. So we said, OK fine, "We'll hire you at this pizza shop but you have to come and be tutored by us in the afternoon." We had a tutoring program and a small business. We tried to link up the academic content of the tutoring program to the business. We taught English by writing up press releases for the business. We taught math by doing the accounting to run the business.

While accurate information is the foundation of effective strategy, learning does not stop once a project has started. Monitoring and evaluating a project's progress or the effects of a personal decision help you understand how your strategy and its implementation may need to evolve or change. Discussing the first year of the tutoring program, James told us:

> It was a great program but it was insufficient. The kids that we were working with were in the worst schools. A lot of them had been kicked out of the regular schools and were in the alternative schools. The regular schools often have enough issues, but the alternative schools were really terrible. And so we said, "Let's try to start our own school."
>
> David and I were co-principals and taught classes. We had twenty kids, five teachers, a counselor and a little row house. We worked from eight in the morning until eleven at night.

In large part because James and his partner took the time to gather information and to analyze the results of their first efforts, the Maya Angelou Public Charter School has been operating successfully for over a decade.

Socio-political Understanding and Action

Beyond information gathering and analysis, strategic understanding must also include an awareness of the politics or power dynamics involved in addressing an issue. It would be ideal if you could simply identify and define a problem, think of an innovative solution, and immediately find support for its implementation. The reality is, however, that there are people who benefit from the status quo and who may have an incentive to work against change. There may also be individuals who want to take advantage of change in a way that you hadn't envisioned. As a result, any strategy must take into consideration the need to work effectively with people whose interests differ from your own. Samantha Yu at the Los Angeles Commission for Children, Youth, and Their Families shared some thoughts on this subject:

> I would tell people to be prepared for the politics....There's nothing that's just pure numbers, just a pure analysis. There is always an intention behind it. As much as we would like to say

> that you need to be impartial, there's always a direction that is driving whatever analysis you're doing....We have to listen as policymakers ask, "How much is it going to cost? Are you going to do it in my district?" As a policy analyst, you're not always prepared to do that....For me, that is probably the thing that was the steepest learning curve.

Both as the director of ACCION and Oxfam America, John often had to navigate political challenges. If, for example, Oxfam took a principled position in one of its campaigns that offended donors or the US government, its ability to fund anti-poverty programs could be threatened.

> When I started as executive director at Oxfam, the Contra War in Nicaragua was devastating that country. Oxfam had launched a number of programs that ran counter to US government foreign policy in Central America. We planned some major advocacy against the Nicaraguan embargo and against the Contra War. I was very concerned that this advocacy would have negative repercussions on our ability to raise money.

Fortunately, John made a concerted effort to explain Oxfam's position to one major donor. After speaking with John, the donor promised to help make up any difference in funding if Oxfam's funding base shrank because of its actions and policies in Central America.

Socio-political awareness is not limited to traditionally "political" situations. Everyone has heard of *office politics*, a term that is usually freighted with negative connotations. Questions of power make many of us uncomfortable. We worry that if we focus too much on politics, keying in on power relationships, we will reduce people from ends to mere means to an end. And, frankly, there are enough real-world examples of this happening that we're right to be concerned and careful. Nevertheless, the reality is that there are vested interests, levers of power, and channels of influence. Being aware of the political landscape is not the same thing as "playing politics." A practical idealist, in order to be practical, must be cognizant of politics and have an ability to formulate strategies that take them into consideration.

Ethical Understanding and Action

Ethical understanding is very much a continuation and extension of our chapter 1 discussion about putting your values into action. It is also the skill most closely tied with the practical idealist's mantra, "choices matter." The term *ethics* can be, in many ways, interchangeable with *values*. *Ethics* can also refer to a code of conduct or a formalized structure based on values. Strategic understanding for a practical idealist must include evaluating the ethical implications of their decisions. This ability to integrate the ethics of your personal life and work with social change is where the rubber really hits the road for your practical idealism.

Reviewing plans and outcomes for ethical consequences is no less a skill than developing political awareness. Ethical analysis occurs before, during, and after a choice. It is an ability that becomes habit only through consistent practice, but it is essential to all practical idealists. Even if you have not studied ethics formally, it might be helpful to know that, at least in Western philosophical frameworks, one, if not all, of the following questions may underpin our ethical decisions.

- What are the consequences of my actions? Who benefits? Should I undertake that which maximizes the most benefits to the most people? Are my actions as beneficial as they can be?
- What is the right thing to do, regardless of the consequences? How would I like to be treated if I were in this situation? What is my duty, my responsibility?
- What are the virtues, characteristics that I value most? Are my actions going to uphold and promote those virtues, such as empowerment and courage?

Practical idealists Amanda Edmonds and Josh Dorfman, for example, have had very different careers, but both brought up the role of ethics in their strategic processes.

Amanda Edmonds is the founder of Growing Hope, a community gardening nonprofit organization that is especially active in under-resourced areas. "Our mission," says Amanda, "is to help people improve their lives and communities through gardening. We work with community groups and schools, at a number of different levels, to use gardening as a vehicle for positive environmental and social change." Even before founding her own nongovernmental organization (NGO), however, Amanda, as a student volunteer in college, was aware of the need to assess the potential ethical implications of her community gardening projects. Amanda was particularly concerned that her projects reflect her commitment to an ethic of sustainability. Prior to starting work on one of her first school gardens, she approached the principal and gave voice to her ethic: "I would like to join *with* you, if you're interested, to put together a team to develop a school garden. My commitment to this garden is that I be a part of it until it can be sustainable without me."

Sustainability encompasses many values in action, including self-reliance, humility, and regard for the environment. Amanda knew that a project that ran only on her energy and enthusiasm would not be as durable nor as effective as a project run by a team from the community. By taking care to consider the project's sustainability, Amanda ensured that a community team could run the garden and educate people about gardening and nutrition indefinitely.

Josh Dorfman founded Vivavi, "an eco-friendly furniture and home-design center," that helps people understand their homes can be fashionable and green. In Josh's case, his ethical understanding emerged from values that developed during the trajectory of his career. Josh had worked in China for the Kryptonite bike lock company, attended business school, and thought he would make a career in business. At a certain point, however, he had what he calls an "environmental epiphany." Josh realized that his initial career goals didn't match his evolving sense of the world and his personal sense of ethics.

> When a billion Chinese people are driving cars that means that there will be five more United States of car drivers on this planet....You talk about unsustainable! For me it's just: "Here's a major problem and I'm going down this path of business and I enjoy what I'm doing but I cannot go take some job that I feel will be doing damage in the long run."

Like Josh and Amanda, practical idealists examine the ethical consequences of their life choices. While sometimes the correlation between a decision and the ethical fallout is quite clear, other times it is not. This is particularly true when making a judgment whether to accept money from what some might consider a tainted source. Late in John's tenure as executive director, for example, Oxfam agreed to accept a $1 million gift from the AES Corporation.

> The AES Corporation was a coal mining company with a new technology for extracting coal. This was a highly controversial donation at Oxfam. Many felt that the organization was selling out to corporate America and argued that Oxfam was providing legitimacy to an environmental polluter. Some colleagues believed that we should reject this donation. This large donation was given to Oxfam to facilitate its work with indigenous populations who were helping to preserve the Amazon. We consulted with our indigenous partners. We consulted with agencies focused on corporate social responsibility. We agreed to the donation because there were no strings attached to the funds other than that we use them in our programs in the Amazon. I traveled to the Amazon with the President of AES Corporation. While there we were able to view some of the oil rigs erected by American corporations to drill oil out of the Amazon. The President of AES heard the arguments of the indigenous people directly. He traveled by canoe to remote areas to talk to indigenous people. Upon his return to the United States, he became an ally for our advocacy work for indigenous people in the Amazon and our lobbying efforts with oil companies in the United States.
>
> Clearly there were trade-offs in the AES fundraising donation. On the one hand, we gave AES credibility and a project they could use in their public relations to claim that they were good citizens. On the other hand, AES provided $1 million to the indigenous populations of the Amazon for them to try to preserve not just the Amazon, but their way of life.

Building Strategic Skills

The ability to visualize all of the various "moving parts" of an issue or problem and then formulate a strategic, political, and ethical response can be developed in many different situations.

Formal education is one key to building broad framework skills. These days a college education is almost a requirement for most jobs, including those in social change fields. A liberal arts education can provide social, economic, and political knowledge, as well as an understanding of philosophical and ethical ideas. It can also provide familiarity with different analytical frameworks that allow you to understand different social issues.

Additionally, while you do not have to have a college or graduate degree to be a practical idealist, graduate school can strengthen your analytical skills and increase your exposure to a particular sector, field, or social issue.

While formal education has a role to play in building strategic skills, work experience and practice using these skills are also essential. Seeing, analyzing, and responding to problems in real life while taking other, sometimes conflicting, interests into consideration can be very different from theoretical study. Remember Samantha Yu? Even with a masters in public policy, she felt her best preparation for the politics of working in Los Angeles city government was...working in Los Angeles city government.

Strategic Understanding

Gathering information, performing analysis, acting strategically, and conducting socio-political and ethical assessments all contribute to your strategic understanding abilities. Strategic understanding requires that you:

- *Know your history.* Look at the history of the issue you want to work on. What have people done in the past to address these issues? What has worked? What hasn't worked? Are there older strategies that were sound but poorly implemented? Is it possible to take the same ideas and create more effective projects?
- *Pay attention to what is happening around you.* Make your own observations and don't stop at amassing facts; perform analysis. Ask people for their comments. Be alert for tacit assumptions. Ask the questions "Why?" and "Why not?"
- *Research the people who are involved in the area you are trying to learn about.* What are their own needs and interests and how

do these elements shape their choices and advocacy? Do the aims of your project or organization overlap with the goals of these other players? Could you work together?

- *Build a comprehensive frame.* What are the different social and political influences that affect the issue you are examining (and vice-versa)? What factors exacerbate or ameliorate the situation? (Making a visual map or flowchart often helps clarify these questions.)
- *Work multi-dimensionally.* Don't just look at the work done on your issue in one field. Are there approaches or models from multiple fields that you can integrate to create a multi-dimensional solution? For example, different models for assessing and addressing global poverty have emerged in fields as various as philosophy, economics, public health, security studies, and politics.
- *Integrate ethical considerations into your actions.* Think about the ethical underpinnings of your project and career actions. Remember to take the time to reassess the ethical implications of what you're doing as you move forward.

PERSONAL AND BEHAVIORAL SKILLS

Personal and behavioral skills include taking risks, taking initiative, active listening, perseverance, and remaining open to new experiences. As we learned in our interviews, not every practical idealist has all these skills—far from it. While, in some cases, our practical idealists seem to be innately gifted with these abilities, in others, they had to work hard to build these personal skills. Wherever you are on the spectrum of ease with the following skills, know thyself! Remember, as we discussed earlier, the importance of taking the time to do just that. Being practical requires understanding who you are, your strengths, your deficits, and your goals. Truthfully, some of these skills may be a struggle to integrate into your life, however, like all things, experience and practice will make it easier.

Taking Risks

After finishing her Presidential Management Fellowship at the Department of Housing and Urban Development in Washington,

DC, Laura Hogshead could have easily transitioned into a job in the federal government with long-term job security. So when she first heard about a possible job at the Center on Poverty, Work, and Opportunity, Laura was uncertain. The center was very new, lacked an established track record, and it was in North Carolina, not in Washington.

> I realized I could see my life so clearly in the federal government. I probably wasn't going to have that many surprises. But I couldn't exactly see what was going on in this life, and I know that I would have regretted not trying. Even though this was less stable, even though it was less certain....When you're young and you have an interesting opportunity, I would encourage anyone to take the chance. It might not always work out the way you thought that it would, and this hasn't worked out the way I thought that it would. It has been very different than I have anticipated, but it has been good.

The practical idealists we spoke with were willing to take risks and move away from what was familiar (literally or figuratively), though some were more comfortable with risk-taking than others. People moved to new cities for work or school, left their home countries to work internationally, and started new businesses and nonprofit organizations. What enabled them to take these risks? In almost every case it was passion about what they were doing and the goals they wanted to achieve. Research consultant Kristen Deremer, who has worked on a variety of international projects, including a study of transitional justice in the Balkans and an assessment of gender programs in Uganda, is clear on the need to take risks:

> I think the most important thing is just to try things out and take risks. Don't be afraid of asking questions and trying out something new, even if you are not sure if you'll be any good at it. My personal experience is that there is value in really putting yourself out there into uncomfortable positions. I do not mean unsafe, but push yourself, go places you wouldn't have thought you would go, physically and emotionally. That

doesn't mean you have to go to Morocco or to Tanzania, but step outside your comfort zone essentially.

We know it's easier for some than others to step out of their comfort zone to that place where growth happens. A high level of commitment to a cause is enough to motivate some to take risks, but it also takes some amount of confidence. Keep in mind that being self-confident is not the same as being an extrovert—although these terms are sometimes erroneously conflated. Confidence, which is from the Latin root *fidere* meaning "to trust," is trusting your abilities and instincts. You might not know how to do something, but you know you can learn. For the practical idealists we interviewed, confidence was grounded in different sources, including a supportive community, education, faith, having succeeded with smaller risks in the past, and watching the successes of other people.

What do you do if you lack confidence? We find it helps to have a partner, parent, or friend who will help you identify your strengths. Sometimes it's hard to see how skilled you are. You may think your accomplishments and abilities are commonplace—nothing special. Maybe you grew up in a family or culture where you were told, "Don't break your arm patting yourself on the back." Sometimes we need to be able to see ourselves through the eyes of our supporters.

UNDERSTANDING YOUR STRENGTHS & CURRENT LIMITATIONS

Consider these questions. If you can, go over your answers with someone who might be able to jog your memory about successes that you may have overlooked or forgotten.

Positive Tools and Experiences at Your Disposal

Think about the different activities that you are engaged in and the ways in which you support the organizations, missions, and individuals in your life. Make a list of what you do or have done on an everyday basis, special accomplishments, and what you think is your general role in your:

- Professional life
- Friends and family life
- Volunteer/public life
- Student life

	Everyday Activities	Special Accomplishments	General Role
Professional			
Friends & Family			
Volunteer/ Public Service			
Student/ Academic			

Imagine you're about to deliver a keynote address and someone is at the podium introducing you. What would they say?

Things to Overcome

- Make a list of your failures and shortcomings. Be honest.
- Are there negatives that you could work on changing that would allow you to take more risks and increase your self-confidence?

Moving Forward

- Look at some of the risks you want to take. What skills or characteristics can help you succeed? What are the gaps that exist between the attributes you have and the ones that you need? Are you sure that everyone who has been successful at taking those risks had the attributes that you listed? (The answer is probably no.) What do you think would happen if you didn't have all those attributes and tried anyway?
- If it was failure, is it irreparable? What magnitude? Can you live with that failure? Most failures become learning experiences and lead to new opportunities.
- Compare your list of negative attributes with your list of accomplishments, skills, and characteristics. Are the negatives really so overwhelming that they would prevent the positives from enabling you to accomplish your goals?
- Look at your community of support. Have you identified reliable members of your personal cheerleading squad who can help you maintain your confidence when you take risks and make daring choices?

If you have answered the questions above and are still feeling less than confident, start small. Set out on less daunting projects or programs where you think you have a really good chance of performing decently. You might try volunteering with an organization that needs your skills or creating your own small-scale initiative.

When Alissa was in college, for example, she and her friend, Amanda, were disappointed that most of their classmates seemed to be in the liberal arts college bubble and lacked an intelligent awareness of international affairs. Talking to strangers wasn't Alissa and Amanda's thing, so sitting at a table asking people to sign a petition or waylaying passers-by to tell them about a specific cause did not appeal to either of them. They knew, however, that they were good at research. Amanda and Alissa decided to write abstracts about international news events that could be posted in places where students would read them. They created the two-person organization *Guerilla Current Events*. Each week they wrote summaries of ten international news stories and printed them on bright orange table tents, which they placed on every table in the college's only dining hall. This non-flashy approach didn't create a groundswell of visible movement on international issues, but it did create a quiet buzz on international news. Amanda and Alissa watched as people picked up the tents and discussed the week's topics. Their organization was later recognized by two campus publications for being a service to the community.

One final word on confidence: When considering your sources of confidence, take a little time to identify whether or not there are people, places, and activities that make you feel stifled, diminished, or incapable. It may be time to leave these things or persons behind.

Humility

Humility may not seem to be a skill, but it can be cultivated. At its best, humility helps you to avoid an arrogance that can impede your ability to get a job, lets you be realistic in your goals, and allows you to see yourself as part of a larger process. Humble practical idealists know they can make a difference but are not too arrogant to recognize when it's time to learn from others.

Allison Greenwood Bajracharya learned to be more humble after her Teach For America work. During the program, Allison overcame a lot of obstacles, which made her feel like she could do anything. She expected that she could be hired as an executive director or a leader of a nonprofit organization. She found, however, that she was offered much more modest positions. After this experience, she thought that young people working to take the lead should "definitely go for it, but also don't be afraid to be humbled, and don't be afraid to go in at the ground level and maybe work for something that you think you're more deserving of." She had gone through an experience that helped her see that there were many people who had valuable skills and knowledge to offer.

Humility in the life of a practical idealist is more than a willingness to start at the bottom. It also means being clear-eyed about the limits of what you can achieve. People who believe they can do everything or know everything often get in the way of people who actually know what they're doing. They gum up the works and start things they cannot finish. One practical idealist, for example, related a story about a "team member" whose intellectual arrogance delayed a report on human security issues. This person's repeated attempts to contribute to areas where he had no educational background or professional experience meant that other team members had to waste time correcting his unsolicited edits and comments.

Humility not only preserves the integrity of the work, it can also protect you from work burnout. Dara Schulbaum is a therapist who works in a partial hospitalization program for youth who struggle with emotional and behavioral problems. She shared this example:

> One day I got off the phone with an insurance company and I was so upset. There's a kid who seems to have everything stacked against him. He was probably born with some bad wiring in the brain; everything went wrong from there, and it seems like it keeps going downhill. I said to the psychiatrist that I work with, "I don't know what we're supposed to do because I don't know how to help him and I don't think we can make any difference in his life." And she responded, "You're not that powerful."

Humility is important, but like any trait it must be balanced. Humility does not mean undervaluing your work, lacking strength of conviction or being short on force of character. On the contrary, humility can go hand in hand with being self-confident, committed, positive, hopeful, and charismatic. A practical idealist leader combines humility with purposeful action, giving credit to others, helping others to build their own skills, and assisting others along their path of personal transformation. Practical idealists believe one person can make a difference and believe that they are such a person. They just also see themselves as part of a larger community working to make change. This understanding of their actions in the context of a larger community may be one of the reasons practical idealists are often humble.

Perseverance and Commitment

One of Alissa's favorite interview quotes is Josh Dorfman's comment about perseverance:

> ...if you get to the point where you're swimming and you're out in the middle of the lake, you can either keep going or turn back. It's the same distance both ways. You have to be the kind of person who is always in the middle of the lake and you're always going to keep going because there are so many points where you would still really rather turn back.

The life of a practical idealist demands perseverance. Right now, part of your perseverance may be working to find a job that responds to your values and passions. Perseverance is also needed to overcome obstacles to accomplishing your job.

Nicole Hoagland, youth programs director at Time Out Youth North Carolina, works with LGBT teens. She helps them to connect with strong support systems as well as educate Charlotte residents about how to be a more accepting community. Nicole loves her job, but it can sometimes feel like an uphill battle. Her organization is only two people so there is a lot to get done all the time. The work is also especially hard since Charlotte is a socially conservative community. Time Out Youth has been the target of anti-gay rhetoric voiced by some members of the community. The weekend before her interview, for example, Nicole and her boss received emails telling them that they were going to go to hell. She says she has her days when she thinks, "Wouldn't it be nice to be somewhere else and have the work be just a little easier because you have broader community support?" She also says, however, "I would guess that a lot of us who are doing this work feel a certain responsibility to do the work *here* because somebody has to." Her commitment to the work getting done means that she is willing to be in a sometimes less than hospitable environment if that's what it takes.

Difficulties will inevitably come up in social change work. Andrea Strimling is another practical idealist. She has had a career working in conflict resolution in the public and nonprofit sectors, is a student of Buddhism, and also writes about practical idealism. In her interview with Alissa, she spoke about the importance of having a strong sense of purpose and commitment. Andrea explains that "many of the world's most inspirational leaders committed to their work so strongly that they were willing to lose their lives to accomplish their goals. Commitment can take many different forms. Whatever its specifics, a sense of purpose, combined with commitment and perseverance, will help you achieve your most important goals." Some of the practical idealists we spoke with have followed social change careers regardless of where their work took them geographically, others have devoted themselves to positions that had small salaries or restricted lifestyles. It's not about dying for your work, but it is, as Andrea said, about commitment and perseverance.

Finally, John, Alissa, and others stress that a vigorous sense of humor can help you persist in trying circumstances. One practical idealist, for example, who worked on the personal staff of a United States senator, was depressed by the mean-spirited and intolerant tone of many constituent letters. One of the things that kept her going was taking the time to read the missives written to the senator on subjects like UFO sightings and inquiries asking the senator to settle an argument as to whether the Pentagon had five or eight sides (yes, that was an actual letter). John says: "I am a proverbial optimist. I see positive coming out of every situation. Humor helps me to maintain that openness."

ORGANIZATIONAL AND DEVELOPMENT SKILLS

Organizational skills allow practical idealists to implement their strategies for addressing the issues they care about. These include technical skills, administrative management, communication, and promotion or "salesmanship." Most of the skills we discuss are transferable from one job to another. Except for the most technical of skills, these abilities are useful in almost any work. Many of John's graduate students are looking for very concrete technical skills—the "how to" of international development. In our experience technical skills *are* important, but no more so than these overall skills that are transferable to almost any practical idealist job or endeavor.

Technical Skills

Technical skills are necessary in every profession and there are, of course, a wide variety of skills that fall into this category. The practical idealists we interviewed were skilled in graphic design, accounting, policy writing, cooking, logistics planning, law, medicine, and playwriting. Technical skills are some of the most practical and concrete components of a practical idealist's toolbox. Whatever field(s) interests you, you will have to know what technical skills you need to have ready on your first day of work.

Jeff Deutsch is the senior graphic designer for Oxfam America. However, he loves art, understands the historical power of an image associated with a cause and has a conscience that leads him to appreciate his work at Oxfam. He told Alissa, "I love graphic design. I can't see myself doing anything else. Graphic design is a good combination of creativity and attention to detail for me. At the end of the day, it's definitely not fine art, it's about communicating an idea. At Oxfam I get to communicate about something that could be literally saving people's lives...." Jeff developed his design skills in the private sector and then was able to contribute his significant experience to Oxfam's communications department. In Jeff's opinion, which is seconded by John, many traditional havens for practical idealists, particularly nonprofits, are becoming increasingly professionalized, insisting that applicants have certain concrete skills when they walk in the door:

> More and more nonprofits are looking for people with a very specific skill set as opposed to people who just have a good heart and want to work at a nonprofit. They're becoming more like a business. If somebody is inclined to work for a nonprofit, then [they need to] learn a skill, learn something concrete. It may not be a specific technical skill like design, web development, or film. It can also be that you are an incredibly good people person and good in the education department or at fundraising and meeting major donors.

At times a particular skill can allow a practical idealist to make ends meet while pursuing work that does not compensate well, if at all. After Paul Buckley received a degree from Earlham School of Religion, he started writing books on Quaker history. Unfortunately, being a historian isn't always that lucrative. So when asked what he did for a living, Paul said, "I spend most of my time as a writer and enough of my time as a statistician to pay the bills."

Another practical idealist, Marie Trigona, works on economic justice issues in Argentina through a media collective that is run in solidarity with factory workers. Her work is very important to her yet it is unpaid. She earns her income by writing about economic justice for print and web news sources. Marie sees her separate job for paying the bills as important in her social change work. It frees her up to do the projects she thinks have the most impact rather than the projects that can get funding.

Like Jeff, Marie also spoke about the power of technical skills in social change work. She is a skilled writer, but she told us that she wished she had another technical trade as well:

> You know what I really regret? I really regret not learning something useful in school professionally. I really regret not having a trade—something to do with manual labor or learning any type of medical skill. I think there's an absolute deficit of professionals who can lend those skills to the movement in a very genuine way. Those skills are absolutely needed. We need accountants! I'm talking about for occupied factories,

> or worker-run cooperatives, microeconomy projects. Communities need a doctor who will provide them with free health care—or a dentist. I really regret what I studied in a lot of ways. In other ways, no, because I am privileged that I make my living by writing. It's a poor living, but it's a living.

Don't fear, however, if you are one of many people who went to a liberal arts college and don't feel like you have technical skills beyond Microsoft Office. One of our practical idealists, Dana Harrison, had held positions in music, teaching, human resources, and financial planning before becoming executive director of Dress for Success Indianapolis. She knew she had strong transferable skills, but she also had some technical knowledge gaps. This has not prevented her from being successful.

> I've taken a couple of workshops, even one week-long workshop to try to fill in what I call my formalized knowledge gaps. I've taken several on fundraising just to help give me a framework and help me internalize the best practices that are out there.

Whether or not you're looking for a job right now, consider the changes you want to see happen in the world and make a list of the technical skills you think would allow you to help bring these changes about. Sometimes these abilities will be the skills that employers look for, which can be found in job descriptions. Other times, you may really need to think outside the box. Look at the issues your field is trying to address and think about the technical skills that might be useful for doing so. It's important to also assess your technical skills that may not be directly relevant but which you've picked up along the way. You never know when they will count. Jennifer Jordan hadn't initially envisioned her math abilities as important for a job in organizing and workers' rights; however, at the Service Employees International Union, Jennifer's job called for "a lot of use of spreadsheets and math to determine whether the hospital has money and if so, how they can allocate it towards wages or healthcare benefits for retirement benefits." Don't underestimate what you bring to the table.

Skills: Planning and assessment questions

- What skills have you used in the past? (Include paid and volunteer work, student life, family life.)
- What skills would enable you to focus on the issues you want to work on in an innovative way?
- What skills do you have that you can't imagine needing in your work? Look again at these skills, you might be surprised where they could fit in.

Administrative Management

Administrative management isn't actually a single skill. It's a group of skills that help an organization operate on a daily basis and succeed over time. Administrative management may include purchasing materials, hiring and firing personnel, administering payroll, developing the organization's advisory board, and long-term planning. For some, performing administrative duties is like putting pieces of a puzzle together—a challenging but satisfying task. Others find them a Sisyphean chore—even when you think you've finished your administrative duties, there are always more to do. Either way, they are a necessary part of any organization's health.

When David Neal and his friends founded the Fair Trial Initiative, an anti–death penalty organization, they were trying to make a difference in the lives of those charged with capital crimes in North Carolina. Their work went well and the organization grew, which increased its administrative needs. David described this increase as the most frustrating part of his job. "Any of those sorts of administrative things are the hardest. It's so important to learn how to do that and get people who are willing to do that." Chris Estes, executive director of the North Carolina Housing Coalition, echoes David's sentiment:

> The challenging stuff is always the organizational development, working with the board, keeping your committees functioning, thinking about fundraising ahead of time, grant writing, cultivating and looking for new opportunities, figuring out things like payroll and financial statements,

> personnel issues, and audits. All that stuff is much more of a challenge for me. Not that I can't do it, but I would prefer to defer to someone else.

And the demand for administrative skills is not limited to those practical idealists who have founded their own nonprofits or who work in management roles. Regardless of where you are on the totem pole or how much you despise paperwork, you have to understand the administrative system under which you operate. Jeff Deutsch, the graphic artist, argues, for example, that some nonprofits practice "too much democracy." In some organizations, the approval process for even minor decisions can become unnecessarily cumbersome, stifling agility and innovation. In order to actually get things done in such an environment you need to look for ways to streamline the process and become savvy as to whose input you really need.

Communication or Articulating Your Passion

Clear communication about your work is vital. Caring about the cause isn't enough. Practical idealists are in the business of change, and change usually involves persuading someone of the need for that change. In all of his practical idealist roles, as employee, executive director, activist, and professor, John found that, day in and day out, in venues large and small, his most called-upon skill was effective communication. John, an extrovert, favors verbal communication; others may choose to focus more on written communication. Whether John was speaking to one person over coffee, two or three people in a meeting, several hundred people at a rally, or a television audience of several million, the fundamentals of this skill remain largely unchanged. Over four decades of practical idealist jobs and endeavors, John has distilled from his experiences what he believes are the key principles to effective public speaking:

Simplicity

What exactly are you trying to say? What is your thesis? Your message must be well-structured, straightforward, and simple. State your main point(s) and supporting arguments clearly. Use plain, jargon-free language unless you're speaking to a specialist audience where your ability to speak their language is the only way they'll accept you. Even then, restate your message in simple language so that they know you can communicate with those outside their community as well.

Once, after John did his first television interview for Oxfam America, his press officer took him aside and told him that in addition to committing a number of television "sins" (wearing a bright white shirt, forgetting to acknowledge the television audience, et cetera), his answers had been too long and too complex for the circumstances. Even when you are trying to communicate a complicated or nuanced position, you need to take care to organize your words so that they are "portable" enough that someone else can take your message and carry it "away" with them.

This is true even for small meetings with just a few colleagues—have a point and stick to it. Think about when you've tried to carry a load of laundry up a staircase without a basket—things, an errant sock, a pair of jeans, are always getting dropped. Just as you need a basket to carry the clothes, you need a simple message to transport your ideas.

Tone

Remember how your parents told you to "Watch your tone"? If your audience takes exception to your tone, chances are they will tune out your message. Speaking on hunger development issues, John learned that it can be difficult to find ways of being provocative and challenging without sounding condescending or too preachy. But, if, for example, you are trying to stir people to action, provoking and challenging them is important—it just needs to be done in deft fashion. Before you speak, consider your end goal. Are you simply offering information? Are you trying to persuade? Are you trying to get people fired up?

Engaging the audience

One way to avoid a disconnect between speaker and audience is to give your listeners a way to participate and become involved in the speech. People do not have to be passive recipients. John has experimented with different ways to get audiences to do more than just listen. One common way is to draw your audience into a dialogue by asking questions and soliciting their responses. If this isn't feasible, look for other ways, even small ones, to include your listeners. For example, in 1995, John gave the commencement address at his alma mater, Denison University:

> I ended my talk by asking the seniors to stand up. I told them that five years from now, they would not remember who had given the commencement address. But I did hope that they would remember that at their graduation they had stood up for justice and against oppression, that they had stood up on their graduation day to say that they would make a difference in the world, and that they would be idealistic in working towards a different world. I challenged them to remember throughout their lives that they had stood up on their graduation day and that they could stand up in the face of injustice and oppression throughout their lives.

Good storytelling

Public speaking is most effective when images are evoked in the listener's mind. At Oxfam, John did a great deal of speaking to students and audiences interested in international development.

> Once at the United Nations, I was at a conference on hunger. Speaker after speaker had droned on about the worsening statistics on poverty and hunger worldwide. I was the last speaker on the panel. The panel moderator asked me to be very brief since the time for the session had run out. I spoke of women I had met in Mozambique just three weeks before. One woman was Antonia, who had escaped a village held by the anti-government guerrillas. She had spent days walking. She had hidden in the woods while a battle raged nearby between government and guerrilla forces. I met her at a feeding camp with her two children. They were all skin and bone. She was eloquent. "It is the war that is killing us and the war is being fueled by arms coming from outside. We don't need food; we need to stop the war. You can feed us today, you can feed us tomorrow. Unless you stop the arms shipments, unless you stop the war, you will have to feed us forever. Give us back peace, we will do the rest."

> The issue was not hunger. The issue was not providing food to millions of people. The issue was the resolve of the international and national communities to help bring about peace, to stop the arms shipments that fueled these wars. I argued that the United Nations needed to help set up the political and economic systems that would get out of the way and allow the resilient, hard-working people of Africa to get on with it.

Focusing on Antonia instead of on abstract concepts was effective public speaking. Boiling the talk down to the essentials and presenting it succinctly and passionately galvanized and energized the meeting.

Repetition
Repeat your main arguments more than once. Many of us just don't get a message the first time we hear it. Human beings tend to remember only a small percentage of what is said, in any case. Repeat your message but don't use the exact same words every time. Changing the language will help people approach your ideas differently and prevent them from tuning out.

Smaller audiences
Speaking to one person or a small group of people requires the same kind of commitment as speaking to a large group. People still need to experience your passion and enthusiasm. In small groups there is often more time so that issues can be dealt with in more depth. Better understanding of an issue often increases the likelihood that your audience will leave the talk and take action on the issue you discussed.

Effective communication with one person and groups, large and small, is a skill that benefits you, not just your listeners. It helps you to sharpen your message, to simplify, and be clear. Preparing to speak allows you to clarify your thinking on a particular subject and gives you the invaluable opportunity to experience people's reactions to your thoughts and ideas.

Promotion and "Salesmanship"
At Oxfam and ACCION, John's communication skills were often used in the service of fundraising or sales. While your job may have nothing

to do with sales or development, many of the same principles apply whether you are courting donors, pitching an idea to an investor, or marketing yourself to an employer. Moreover, many practical idealist initiatives depend on convincing others to contribute their time and money to a particular program or cause. If you work at a nonprofit or another institution that is largely dependent on grants and donations, you probably understand just how fraught this prospect can be.

John puts it this way:

> All organizations in the nonprofit, public, and private sectors may face the need to raise funds. Whether you're convincing someone to invest in an idea in exchange for the satisfaction of making the world a better place and a tax break, or in exchange for a larger profit later, you are asking someone to fork over their money. Some organizations have set people who play this role, while others may encourage a diverse array of people to assist in raising funds for their own projects. Learn about fundraising, whether or not it is a specific component of your job. It is essential to keeping an organization alive, and if you advance through the organization and take on more responsibilities, it is an activity that you will come into contact with. Even those who are never responsible for fundraising can be helpful to fundraisers by giving the fundraisers pertinent information about the projects for which money is needed.

Some of us would rather fill our pockets with rocks and walk into a river than sell anything. Maybe you never joined your high school band because you knew sooner or later you'd wind up having to sell oranges or candy bars. Nevertheless, understanding the process and learning the keys to successful sales is part of being a practical idealist—even if you're only selling your ideas. Fortunately, even if you are not a natural at sales and promotion, there are sales and fundraising techniques that can be learned.

Believe

The first step to selling anything is believing in the product. You have to believe that what you are selling is good and worthwhile. This is a first step but certainly not a sufficient step. There are many worthwhile products, many worthwhile social goals. You have to make yours stand out. A corollary to understanding and believing in your product is enthusiasm. It is hard to convince someone else to "buy something" if you are unenthusiastic, apologetic, or vague. It is, therefore, important to practice your communication skills, including expressing yourself clearly and concisely and looking directly into people's eyes.

Listen

Remember to listen and let the potential donor, colleague, or investor speak about what's important to them. You both know that you are selling something, whether it is your organization, a project, an idea, or your own abilities. Your product, however, may have several aspects to it. The buyer might be interested in one particular aspect of what you are selling. It is essential for you to key in to that facet and make sure that the donor realizes that your product does fit his or her most pressing need. If, for example, you are fundraising for a nonprofit or lobbying in the public sector for a program that encompasses gender, community participation, agriculture, and advocacy, then you have an array of program components that might be of interest to that buyer. It is up to you to keep bringing up new ideas until you see the buyer become excited about one of them.

Exude confidence

It is also important for you to exude confidence, not desperation. Money attracts money. People like to be involved in programs that are going to be successful, programs that have attracted others already. Even if it is your first potential sale, you need to be resolute that the money will be raised, the product will be made, and the project will be successful.

Build a relationship

If you are going to have a continuing interaction, work on building a relationship of trust and mutual confidence. This means saying "I don't know" rather than risking inaccuracy. This means being honest about what worked in the past and what did not work. Establishing trust also means getting to know the individual beyond the donor. If you're fundraising, it may mean getting to know the families of the donors, remembering details about their kids, visiting people in their homes, and taking the time to get to know the interests, needs, and wants of the individual. This can be rewarding and over time you build friendships with your clients, with your supporters.

Timing

Just as it is difficult to sell bathing suits in December, it is also hard to sell an idea or a proposed action at the wrong time.

> During the height of the anti-apartheid movement in the United States, Oxfam America decided not to focus on South Africa. Instead, we decided to launch a campaign on Namibia. Namibia, adjacent to South Africa, had suffered under South African rule. When it became independent from South Africa, it needed strong support from the international community to undertake the transition to democracy and effective development. Oxfam felt that it should try to expand the focus in the United States from just apartheid within South Africa to include this new and emerging state of Namibia. Oxfam launched a major campaign, but Americans were interested in apartheid in South Africa, not in Namibia. I remember at a television station in San Francisco, I interviewed on the nightly news as part of our Namibia campaign. The local host did not have time to talk to me at all before we went on the air. Her first question to me was, "You are here to talk about Namibia. Is this some kind of a fruit only grown in Africa?" Namibia was not part of the consciousness of the United States. The timing of the campaign was wrong and it flopped dismally.

CONCLUSION

Centuries ago, guild workers advanced through the stages of apprentice, journeyman, and master as their skills increased. The system was premised on incremental but constant improvement. Today, in a world where many of the tools we use, particularly software, change almost constantly, it's difficult not to be a little envious of medieval stonemasons and their tools that remained unaltered over a lifetime. There were no patches to download for their mallets, no operating system upgrades for their chisels. Nowadays, except, perhaps, in the world of athletics and the arts, there are few ready examples of accumulated skill and eventual mastery. Nevertheless, strategic, personal, and technical skills, while less tangible than an ability involving wood or stone, when practiced consistently, can yield a mastery both substantial and subtle. In the end, you may not raise a cathedral, but you will create your own practical idealist masterwork.

3. Work and Jobs

Allison works for the Los Angeles Unified School District; Peter has a job at the Timberland Company; Marie writes for progressive media organizations; Sasha manages his nonprofit, Mapendo International; Jeff does graphic design at Oxfam America; Rob instructs teachers at Indiana University; Tambra performs and teaches African dance in Atlanta; and Rachel counsels youth affected by HIV/AIDS in Boston.

The work of a practical idealist lies at the intersection of "What do I want to do?" and "Where can I be helpful?" It's as diverse as the people who choose to ask those questions. We find practical idealists in government, the private sector, nonprofits—in all categories of work and life. Now that you've thought about your values, your passion(s), and the skills that you are starting out with, it's time to think more directly about the specific kinds of work you want to do. This chapter focuses on the places practical idealists work and finding or creating the type of work you want to do.

As a practical idealist, where you work will be determined by your passions and values, but keep in mind where you work will likely change many times. Your career may take you from a job at a nonprofit to a corporate position or from the private to the public sector (government) and vice versa. The crossover between government and other sectors is not just for lobbyists. There are plenty of folks who move from the profit to nonprofit world, from education to media, or from government to a law firm.

As we described in the previous chapter, Laura Hogshead left her position at the Department of Housing and Urban Development (HUD) to pursue a job at the Center on Poverty, Work and Opportunity. Laura had begun working at HUD as a Presidential Management Fellow right out of graduate school. She stayed for three years and then moved to the newly created center at the University of North Carolina. Both positions worked on poverty issues but in different ways. She believed this transition would be a good opportunity to expand the reach of her work.

Many practical idealists work in both the nonprofit and public sectors during their careers. People doing direct service or policy work in one sector may leave to do the same type of work in another. It is also not uncommon for those doing direct service work at a nonprofit to transition into governmental policy work with the goal of achieving social change on a systemic level. There are also many, many jobs—accountant, graphic designer, lawyer, editor, et cetera—that are not confined to one sector but are found in the public, private, and nonprofit sectors. Moreover, no bright line separates the profit and nonprofit, private and public spheres. Nonprofits manage profitable ventures; private businesses run foundations; private contractors do government work.

For each of the three major employment sectors, we have assembled an inventory of questions that you should try to answer when considering a position. Responding to these questions will take thought and research on your part. While these lists may at first appear onerous, it really is a question of "pay now or pay later." If you don't thoroughly reflect and investigate prior to choosing a sector or accepting a position, you may very well find yourself in a job that is neither personally satisfying nor expressive of your practical idealism.

Direct Service or Policymaking

If you are thinking about employment with a nonprofit or in the public sector, one of the first questions that you need to consider is whether a direct service or policymaking job best suits your temperament and ambitions. Do you want to work one-on-one with clients—people with some need? Would you find the concrete results of direct action work more fulfilling than a policy position? Or would you prefer to do research, write position papers, and be involved in policymaking and systemic change? Would you, for example, rather be a high school teacher or an education policy analyst for a local government? Or do you want a job that allows you to help on an individual and systemic level?

When John applied to graduate school, he applied to divinity school and an international relations program. In his mind, he saw the choice between direct pastoral work and policymaking as stark. The reality was not so simple. With a degree from a divinity school, he could have become a policy analyst or political activist and promoted civic change. With an international relations degree, by contrast, he could still be on the front lines, providing direct relief to disaster victims or arranging micro loans or community development services overseas. John eventually chose to get his masters and doctoral degrees in international relations, but he has, even while an executive director of nonprofits, maintained a commitment to helping individuals in tangible, measurable ways.

Dara Schulbaum is a therapist who works in a partial hospitalization program for youth who struggle with emotional and/or behavioral problems. She loves her job, but has plans to shift both the type and the sector of her work while maintaining a focus on youth. After spending years as a therapist, Dara wants to work for an organization that helps to address the larger social issues that affect the children in her program. This move is also part of her burnout prevention strategy. Policy work allows Dara to advocate for change while taking a break from the emotional demands of direct service. Moreover, her direct service experiences have given her genuine insight into the issues faced by children and families with special mental health needs and have made her a credible and articulate advocate on their behalf.

The question of policymaking versus direct action confronted Laura Hogshead while she was working on her masters of public administration at the University of North Carolina. Laura told Alissa that she had considered going into direct service work as a social worker after graduation, but certain volunteer experiences convinced her otherwise:

> What I realized through working at several homeless shelters and volunteering at several places was that I am not the best

> person to have on the frontline. I am a crier; I'm a handholder and I'm not very good at the tough love and saying "no." A mentor of mine, who is a social worker, said "Laura, you have to understand what your temperament is, and you also have to understand what level of change you want to be on. You can be one social worker and help client after client after client. But if your temperament is more policy-oriented, you could work on policies that would change the lives of thousands of families at once." So you have to decide where on that continuum you want to be.

If you work at a nonprofit or in the public sector, chances are you will eventually have to choose between more hands-on work and relatively removed administrative tasks. Particularly within nonprofits, employees tend to start out in a programmatic position and receive promotions into positions that are more focused on management and organizational development. For example, John started out in Costa Rica working directly on community development programs. After two years, he was offered two jobs. The first position was managing an urban development program in Ecuador—a program directly focused on the deliverables of the organization. The second job involved relocating to agency headquarters in order to become executive director—a management position removed from the provision of direct services. Organizational development and management in a nonprofit can include strategic planning for the organization, fundraising, working with the board, et cetera. Likewise in the public sector, an administrative position may entail institutional planning and lobbying for a larger slice of the budget, as well as managing other employees.

Although moving from program work to administration is common in the nonprofit world, it is not the only path. Dana Harrison, the executive director of Dress for Success Indianapolis, for example, is an exception to the program-to-administrative-work progression. She became a nonprofit executive even though she didn't have a lot of experience in nonprofit organizations. During the job search in which she landed her current position, she realized that she would enjoy and would be good at nonprofit administration. Dana clearly relishes her administrative and development responsibilities:

> As the executive director I am responsible for making sure all of the wheels stay on. We're driving a big vehicle here and there are a lot of wheels. I'm not on that frontline with the clients. I'm behind the scenes helping to set strategic direction, do the long-term and even some of the short-term planning, and of course, the fundraising, the community awareness.

While Dana's choice was quite deliberate, Alissa and John have both known a number of people in nonprofit and public sector leadership positions who didn't begin their careers to work as fundraisers, write budget proposals, and hire staff, but wound up doing just that. These practical idealists had begun with a mission to try to help kids reduce violence in their lives, help families find housing and navigate government assistance systems, or help reduce poverty through top-notch research. Some people are happy with this switch to administrative work, but others are not. Before taking on a new position, you need to think about what will be required and whether that's really what you want to do. In management jobs you might make more money or have increased responsibilities, but you may lose the ability to do the direct service work that motivated you in the first place. You may be okay with that, but for some this transition means that they lose what sustains their practical idealism.

A friend of ours once personally tended many of the public garden spaces for a town in the West. Her responsibilities included caring for a rose garden that contained over 1,000 rose bushes as well as other showcase gardens. Since she was a talented landscape artist and designer, her boss kept attempting to promote her, but Irene did not want a job that kept her away from her beloved outdoors. She accepted additional managerial duties but fought to be able to continue to work outside. When a promotion was finally forced on her, she stayed on for two stressful, miserable years and then quit to start her own landscaping business.

Similarly, after John moved into a management role, he missed the direct service work with people in the field. His eventual solution was to resign as director of ACCION International, work on urban community change in the United States for two years, and spend a year in the Dominican Republic. Later, as a director at both Oxfam America and the Famine Center, he insisted on spending time in the field so that he could continue to connect directly to the people who benefited from the missions of the organizations.

Working in a Nonprofit Organization

The types and kinds of nonprofits, both national and international, are so diverse that the term *nonprofit* is about as helpfully descriptive as the words *business* or *corporation*. Such is their variety that the only commonality between many nonprofits is their tax-exempt status and their governance by an independent board of directors. For instance, some nonprofits are funded primarily by grants and membership fees while others rely on compensation received in return for services they provide. For example, Oxfam America and Mapendo depend mostly on grants, whereas private, not-for-profit hospitals and some community social service agencies depend on fees and payments.

A more useful distinction, though still broad, is the divide between the nonprofit organizations that focus primarily on providing direct help to people and those that concentrate heavily on policymaking and advocacy. Organizations that focus on direct service activities include nonprofits like Second Helpings, which works on culinary training and provides food to public organizations, and Dress for Success, which provides business clothes and job search counseling to women transitioning into the workforce. Nonprofits that primarily focus on policymaking and advocacy include organizations like the Center on Poverty, Work and Opportunity, which focuses on domestic poverty issues. Even so, many nonprofits pursue both. One such example is the Mexican American Legal Defense Fund (MALDEF), which has direct service programs, like parent trainings, and also performs advocacy work.

Direct action or policymaking, program work or administration—these are just two of the choices involved in selecting an appropriate nonprofit position. John, who has worked for decades in nonprofits, has assembled a brief list of questions for those of you considering working for a nonprofit or setting one up (more on that later).

Questions to ask and points to consider before working at a nonprofit organization:

1. All nonprofits are not equal. Do due diligence on yours.
   a. Some are big and bureaucratic, some small; some are monopolies and powerful, others are basically irrelevant. What is the reputation of your nonprofit?
   b. Are you comfortable with the scope or reach of your organization? Does it concentrate on a neighborhood, city, state, nation, or region, or is it international in scope?
   c. Are you comfortable with how the organization views its clients, customers, beneficiaries, end-user stakeholders? For example, do they see them as victims to be rescued or owners of their own personal and community development?
   d. Some nonprofits are political (but not necessarily partisan), whereas others ignore the political implications of their work. Some are invested in systemic change and others advocate for existing institutions. What is the mission statement of the organization?
   e. Many nonprofits are diligent about transparency and accountability; others are rarely evaluated on meeting their social justice goals. Does the nonprofit have strong internal accountability measures in place?
2. Can you work for the social bottom line, which is not always quantifiable? At a poorly managed nonprofit, objectives and goals are often not clear; however, even effective organizations may find it hard to quantify results. It's possible, for example, to count the number of dollars raised and amount of aid distributed, but what about policy change? It's difficult and expensive to completely quantify (at least immediately) the effects of reduced carbon emissions or increased community education programs.
3. Can you work for less? Nearly all nonprofit jobs pay less than their corporate counterparts. (Less doesn't necessarily mean very little, but it is less.)
4. Can you tolerate the internal agency culture? Organizational customs and attitudes vary enormously. If a nonprofit places a

strong emphasis on making sure its internal procedures sync with its overall mission, will you likely find this relevant and necessary or endless navel-gazing?

5. Nonprofits were once run mostly by volunteers, but they have become more professional. Can you work in an organization with volunteers who may not deliver? Can you work in an organization that has become so professionalized that it has lost its informal and collegial culture and even, perhaps, the original passion of its founder?
6. Is the organization really a nonprofit or is it for all intents and purposes a quasi-governmental agency? Some organizations get all or most of their money from government; how independent is it?
7. Is the "nonprofit" actually a profit-making venture? Some nonprofits charge fees and survive on the "profit" made by selling a service.
8. How binding is the mission statement to the board, the staff, and donors? Does institutional preservation and survival trump all?
9. What are the politics of the agency? What is its philosophy of work, of development? Who wins and who might lose from its work?
10. Are you sure that your personal mission and idealism can be expressed in this nonprofit environment with the colleagues you would have and within the established organizational culture? Will your values and ethics be reflected in the agency? Will you be living out your own mission and practical idealism at work?

Working in a Private Business

Practical idealists can focus on social change issues in the private sector in a multitude of ways. They help businesses minimize their environmental footprint, follow fair trade practices, and make products in a socially responsible way. As a practical idealist, you might choose to work for a business that makes a product that benefits a community in need or for a company that focuses on providing services for nonprofits or the public sector. Some companies, for example, do solid international development and relief work via contracts with the US government.

There is a wide variety of jobs that practical idealists in the for-profit sector can perform that make a real difference. Kenan Bigby, for example, works in Boston as a project manager at Trinity Financial.

He oversees the development of building projects to revitalize neighborhoods. Trinity, which builds mixed-income housing, works to minimize the negative impacts of real-estate development by including a wide array of stakeholders in its processes. Peter Girard is employed as a senior analyst on the Environmental Stewardship Team at the Timberland Company. He assesses the environmental footprint of the company's business units and helps to focus its resources on environmental programs. Among other things, his job includes developing environmental performance metrics, conducting lifecycle analysis of footwear and apparel, and helping his company put this information to use. Sanchia Patrick is a product manager for the North American division of the medical device and services provider Coloplast Corporation. Coloplast, which was founded in Denmark, has clearly articulated policies regarding transparent corporate governance, business conduct, and environmental and social responsibility. In addition to her work at Coloplast, Sanchia is the co-founder of Baby Peaches, a nonprofit that supports expectant mothers and newborns.

Questions to consider:

1. What kind of bottom line would you like your employer to work for? Could you work for a company that:
   a. integrates social and/or environmental concerns into its decision-making, even if this means a lower profit margin and/or slower growth;
   b. generally places greater importance on profits than social and environmental concerns; or
   c. is exclusively focused on the bottom line?
2. Does the impetus behind the company's creation matter to you? Some businesses are started by people who want to "do good" and see a business as a means to implement their plans. Other businesses are started by people who want to have a business and use socially responsible ideas or provide goods and/or services to the nonprofit sector purely as a business strategy.
3. Do you feel comfortable with what the company charges clients who may be nonprofits, governments, or nonwealthy individuals?

4. In terms of a daily work environment, how would you feel about being either the lone individual, or in the lone office, that represents social and environmental issues in your company?
5. What kind of internal accountability measures do you want to see, particularly with respect to social change goals (if there are any)? What do others, including the media, say about your company?
6. Private companies can have vastly different corporate cultures. Are you more of a traditional business suit, business casual polo shirt, or Jimmy-Buffett-Hawaiian-shirt kind of person? While these labels apply to clothes, they also relate to the ways in which people communicate and the levels of protocol and structure in one's business life.
7. Can your personal mission and idealism be expressed in this environment, with the colleagues you would have, and within the established organizational culture?

Working in the Public Sector

While some practical idealists from the business or nonprofit sectors work indirectly for governments as contractors, others are employed directly by a government department or agency at the local, state, or federal level. Brandie Ishcomer was employed by the library system of the City of Phoenix and Samantha Yu does policy analysis for the City of Los Angeles. Professor James Forman, Jr., was once a public defender in Washington, DC. Laura Hogshead worked to make better housing more accessible to low-income people while working at the Department of Housing and Urban Development. While outsourcing and contract work has become increasingly common at the federal level, the number of jobs in the public sector remains large. State social workers, Centers for Disease Control scientists, public schoolteachers, politicians, and government bureaucrats are all public servants, and the public sector offers many opportunities for practical idealists.

Questions to consider:

1. Find out as much as you can about the agency. Do its work and work habits seem to fit you? Like nonprofits, some government offices are huge, while others are small; some dominate with

respect to certain policy issues or control certain services while others have little influence over policy or are very limited in their responsibilities and powers.

2. Is the agency diligent about transparency? Is it considered effective in its work? Agencies may be reviewed by other government offices, but they are rarely evaluated in terms of social justice goals. Does your agency or department have strong internal accountability measures in place?
3. What is the scope or reach of your organization? For example, a local government might have an office that is attempting to revitalize its downtown business district while a federal program might do assessments and disburse funds for cleaning up brownfields and other sites of urban blight. What scope attracts you?
4. Can you tolerate the internal agency culture? Government is by definition bureaucratic. Do you feel comfortable working in that setting? Will you be able to keep your excitement in the face of rules you may not be able to change?
5. Despite bureaucratic structures, customs and attitudes can still vary depending on the office. Offices at the local, state, federal, and intergovernmental levels may be different, and management and leadership have an impact on office culture. What do you know (or what have you heard) about your office?
6. Are the people who work in the office burnt out or is there an air of energy that people bring to their work? One practical idealist, recalling a stint working for the National Institute on Drug Abuse (NIDA), reported that while some of the secretaries tried to do as little work as possible (and even told her to bring a book to work), others at NIDA were enthusiastic, committed, and relentlessly hard-working.
7. Can you work for the social bottom line, which is not always quantifiable? Do you know if your objectives and goals will be decided by bureaucrats outside your office who have little knowledge of your actual work?
8. Can you work for less money? While some professional positions (attorneys, scientists, engineers, et cetera) and the upper grades of federal service tend to be relatively well-compensated with good benefits and decent pensions, the yearly salaries of

government employees never reach the highest amounts offered in the private sector.

9. How is your office's standing with the current administration? Do they generally give adequate funding to your office and its programs?
10. Do you know how much a change in administration or shift in congressional control has tended to affect the programs and funding for the office(s) where you want to work?
11. What are the politics of the agency? What is the philosophy of its work? Who wins and who might lose from its work?
12. Are you sure that your personal mission and idealism can be expressed in this environment, with the colleagues you would have, and within the established organizational culture?

Build Your Own Job

Often when people think of creating their own job, they assume this means starting a nonprofit or a business, but it can also mean finding where there is a gap within an existing organization and proposing a project that would fill that gap. For example, in response to a disconnect between an NGO's program and the people that program is intended to help, you might conceive of a new outreach and education program. If your project idea is good enough and the organization has a strong development team, they might accept your offer and work to get funding for the program (and your salary). If not, you might be able to get their permission to raise the money yourself while partnering with them.

Funding your proposed work within an organization needs to be done systematically:

- Research potential funding sources, whether individuals or organizations, and if appropriate, meet with them to see whether your work project falls within their funding parameters.
- Contact the person in charge of the work that interests you. You will need to explain your work interest, preparation for doing the work, and your ideas for getting funding. The organization needs to know that you will be a help rather than a chore to include in its programs. Just because your labor is "free," that doesn't mean it won't cost them. Working with you requires taking time away

from other tasks, and, if they agree to a partnership, they are putting their organization's creditability on the line.

- Work with your organization of interest to get the actual funding. Who you work with on fundraising will depend on the organization's size and division of labor. You'll want to make sure that you can use the organization's name and fiscal status in your fundraising strategy. The organization may leave most of the fundraising work up to you or be very involved in the process. Your strategy may include soliciting donations from individuals, foundations, and various levels of government—any source with money. It is crucial, however, that you secure the organization's approval before approaching any of their already established donors. Organizations need to protect their funding streams, and you need to take care that your initiative will not hurt their existing programs.

One method of getting money to fund your job within an organization that will not conflict with an organization's fundraising is a fellowship. There are a number of foundations that provide fellowships to individuals to work at an institution of their choice. Sometimes an individual may apply for the fellowship and indicate the organization where they would like to work and the project they would like to pursue. Other times, an individual and an organization apply together. In either case, you have to be in contact with the organization and think about work that you could do before you apply.

Sasha Chanoff, who runs Mapendo, an organization that works with refugees, was able to fund a staff person through the Academy for Educational Development New Voices Fellowship. This program offers multiple fellowships in diverse areas including human rights, workers' rights, education equity and reform, migrant and refugee rights, and racial justice and race relations. Additional examples of fellowships won by practical idealists include the Soros Justice Advocacy Fellowship and the Reprieve Fellowship. The former is given for innovative policy advocacy projects that impact one of the Soros Foundation's criminal justice priorities. The latter is given to people to work on anti–death penalty endeavors in the United States or Caribbean.

Practical idealists can also potentially build their own jobs within the public and private sectors as well, but the requirements for doing so differ. For example, let's say you worked in state government for an office that manages that state's State Children's Health Insurance Program (SCHIP). You might come up with an innovative outreach program to help make sure that children who were eligible for SCHIP were actually enrolled. You would then need to convince your supervisors of the need for this new program, why it would work, and why they should secure a budget for it. You would also have to persuade them that you had the knowledge and skills to develop and manage this new program.

There are also opportunities for you to craft your own innovative job within the private sector. Start-up companies are usually small, flexible, and open to experimentation. Some multinationals have an ethos of experimentation and innovation. Here again you have to sell your idea to your boss, your manager, the owner, or whoever can give you the green light to explore a new idea. As you probably gather, these are not easy things to do and much depends on the internal culture of the government office or business.

Creating Your Own Organization

Instead of partnering with an existing organization, some practical idealists want to start their own nonprofit or business from scratch. Their reasons vary. Some may simply want to be in charge of seeing their new idea bloom or they may be convinced that achieving their goal requires a new, independent organization. What these founders sometimes do not realize, however, is that they will have to spend most of their time on fundraising, management, planning, and organizational development. Sasha Chanoff, for example, built the nonprofit Mapendo from the ground up. Before going to graduate school, he had worked with Sudanese refugees in Africa. He saw that the existing refugee resettlement system did not work well and felt there was a need for a nonprofit that would focus on refugees who were forgotten by the international system. Sasha used John's NGO management class to develop his business plan and after graduation set up Mapendo. He struggled through the first year with little money and way too much work. As a result of his determination and drive, however, by year three Sasha had celebrity participation and had raised enough money to serve forgotten refugees in Nairobi's urban slums. During this period, he devoted his whole life, night and day, to making Mapendo a success. The same caveats hold true if you start your own small business. If you create your own company, you will need to find capital and investors, manage the growth of the business, and identify contractors and suppliers that match your business model and social ethos.

Though a number of the practical idealists we spoke with had established their own organizations, they had differing opinions about encouraging others to do likewise. Amanda Edmonds, who started Growing Hope, an NGO that promotes community gardens in Ypsilanti, Michigan, acts as an advisor at her local nonprofit resource center. Amanda stresses that people need to think seriously about the costs of starting a new organization. Before creating a new nonprofit, she recommends asking, "How can you use the [community's] existing resources to become a part of something or for the first five years be part of [an already existing organization] so that you can really focus on doing your work as opposed to designing network computer systems or your database or those sorts of things?"

Another of our practical idealists, Elizabeth Ouzts, moved back to North Carolina to revive the defunct North Carolina Public Interest Research Group (PIRG). She had worked for PIRG in New Jersey, and when Elizabeth restarted NCPIRG, she had the organizational support of the national PIRG. Her coordinator, however, was based in Atlanta, so Elizabeth was in charge of developing all of the programs within North Carolina. Through her work, she was able to "build support in the State General Assembly to act to extend the ban on new hog farms being built." Later on, she separated from NCPIRG to start Environment North Carolina because she felt there was a need for an organization that focused exclusively on environmental issues. Elizabeth now manages a small staff and is a significant player on environmental issues in the state.

While there are benefits to having support from an already existing organization, we have also interviewed practical idealists who look back very fondly on starting their own entirely new organization without such support. In the case of Josh Dorfman, founder and president of Vivavi, the business he wanted to open was clearly new and different. He had been to business school and spent time working in both small and large businesses. Josh's passions and experiences meant that he was both committed to and prepared to start a new enterprise.

There was no consensus among our practical idealists about whether or not it was a wise move to strike out on one's own. Josh Dorfman and Sasha Chanoff encouraged others to start new ventures and insisted that if someone was excited by an idea and felt that they could make it happen, she should go for it. Others stressed the benefits of working within an established organization or company. In the end, it is a personal decision, but one that must be based on a clear-eyed understanding of the need for your service or product, a realistic assessment of the amount of money needed to start and sustain your endeavor, and a willingness and ability to fundraise, manage yourself and others, and immerse yourself in the sometimes tedious details of running a business or nonprofit.

Exploring Different Fields

Anyone who's ever walked into a coffee shop and been confronted by thirty kinds of coffee drinks and twenty types of tea knows that sometimes there's such a thing as too many choices. Nonprofit or for-profit business? Private or public sector? Administrator or program implementer? Before selecting a job or sector from the big menu, it obviously helps to get at least a small taste of what's on offer. Many of our practical idealists used internships and summer work to sample their choices. Others used fellowships to bolster their resumes and get the flavor of, for example, work in a government agency. Taking on volunteer responsibilities is yet another way to try a new kind of work or area. Volunteering is a particularly good option for those who can't afford to live on an intern's stipend or already have a full-time job.

Summer work, internships, fellowships, and volunteering are all ways to gain experience in a field without making a long-term commitment and often without having a lot of prior experience in the field. Remember, too, that these opportunities aren't just for students or recent graduates. They are not limited to structured programs with formal application processes—instead they can be flexible and informal. They can be full- or part-time; last a few weeks or a couple of years; and be paid, unpaid, or done in exchange for a non-cash benefit like studio time, free instruction, or room and board. The diversity of opportunities is tremendous, and they all can open up new possibilities.

Internships and Fellowships

There are a lot of internships and fellowships out there. Some can be easy enough to find as they are listed at career centers, on job boards, in local libraries, and on websites like idealist.org, Net Impact's job board, the Foundation Center's Philanthropy News Digest, or the US government job website, usajobs.gov. Unlike fellowships, many internships are informal and unlisted. For this reason, it's a good idea to contact the organizations that you're interested in and ask if they have any openings. Jennifer Jordan, for example, interned at the government affairs firm Smith, Dawson and Andrews. Her internship was unstructured and created on an ad hoc basis, but gave her substantive duties that allowed her to make a real contribution. The experience was so positive, Jennifer decided to return to Washington, DC, when she graduated from college.

The types of places that accept interns vary widely. They include NGOs of all sizes, government offices and agencies, intergovernmental organizations like the UN, and for-profit businesses. Depending on the size of the organization, there may be different application processes. Some will ask you to apply directly to the program officer or manager you'd be working under. Others route your application through a human resources department and rely on that office to determine where your skills will be of most use. If you join a large intern pool that gets farmed out to one of a number of offices, consider contacting the office or project whose work holds the most interest for you and ask if they'd be willing to request that you work for them.

Our practical idealists confirmed that the most important thing about an internship is to have a supervisor who gives you substantive work. If you feel that you can do more, then work on doing a good job with what you have and then ask for more. Alissa was once in an internship where she found out after a few weeks that her boss never gave out work but had to be asked for assignments. During Araceli Simeón Luna's internship at MALDEF, she learned she could take on more program-related duties and people would appreciate her drive and initiative. This is not, however, always the case. At another organization, Araceli discovered that doing anything beyond the scope of her assigned administrative duties was not taken well. As an intern, you'll need to find out how supervisors may respond to your initiative and willingness to go above and beyond your appointed tasks.

While the line distinguishing scholarships, internships, and fellowships can be somewhat blurry and the terms are often used interchangeably, fellowship programs tend to be for individuals with advanced degrees or who already have significant professional experience. After finishing her masters in public administration, Laura Hogshead won a two-year paid fellowship from the Presidential Management Fellows Program. Following grad school and military service, Eric Greitens, got "an incredible education in how policy is created in the United States" through a White House Fellowship. A number of professional organizations and philanthropic institutions also offer fellowships within congressional offices. Other practical idealists we interviewed received intensive training in public service and leadership through the Jane Addams–Andrew Carnegie and Coro Foundation fellowship programs. The Coro Foundation, for example, offers a nine-month "experiential leadership training program" that allows people to participate in public service while coming together to discuss ideas that are intrinsic to their work. There are also fellowships affiliated with colleges and universities for which fellows gain access to mentors, money to travel, and other educational opportunities.

We can't emphasize enough the benefits of gaining exposure to different fields. As in all things, it will take some effort on your part, however. Graphic designer Jeff Deutsch told us how one summer during college he "literally went through the phone book, contacting design firms to see if they wanted an intern to work for free." He continues, "I found a small family-run studio and they said, 'Sure, you can work for us for free.' I went in and saw what they do and what design was and realized I was really interested in it." Following his summer experience, Jeff took some design classes in college, and "I was sold, I knew it. I knew this was it for me. I totally fell in love with it."

Volunteering

Volunteering was another way that our practical idealists gained work experience, networked, and explored new fields. Alissa, for example, became well-versed in community development work as a volunteer. Each summer during college she worked on a project called Bronxfest, hosted by Roberto Clemente State Park in the Bronx. The festival brought together performers, visual artists and social service organizations for the community. As co-organizer of the Children's Corner (CC), she attended organizing committee meetings, planned the CC activities, managed CC volunteers, and both oversaw and facilitated activities on the day of the event. The work was enjoyable and fulfilling, but it also connected Alissa to organizations doing community development work in New York City, since many of the committee members represented nonprofit and public sector offices. Alissa could have used these ties to find work in New York, but her plans took her elsewhere. Instead, she used committee members as recommenders for her application to do community development and peace-building work in inner-city Indianapolis.

Other practical idealists were able to parlay their volunteer connections into paying jobs. After college, Annie Sartor, a community organizer for Oceana, moved to San Diego without a job. When asked how she found work, she said that volunteering was key. "You go to meetings, you volunteer, especially getting into the nonprofit world, you have to volunteer. I was new in town, and I had friends who had volunteered for organizations, and I was involved in a lot of different issues continuing on my [political] bent."

Volunteering can prove particularly helpful for those with limited experience in a particular area who want to learn more. Some of our practical idealists found that the camaraderie created by a group of people who are giving of their time can lead to informal mentoring relationships as well. The opportunities and types of volunteer work are almost endless. Some groups need the sort of help that requires very little special training while other organizations actively seek volunteers who can contribute specialized services pro bono. In any case, however, it's important to remember that even though you're not being paid, you are making a commitment that cannot be broken lightly. Many nonprofits rely on the work of their volunteers, and volunteers who don't fulfill their obligations threaten the integrity, if not the survival, of the organization.

Of course, even if you're not looking to learn about a new field or career, you can still be a volunteer. At times, this may mean using a skill from your day job as an accountant, graphic designer, or paralegal to help a nonprofit, government agency, or business working towards social responsibility. At others, your volunteer work may be completely different from what you do from nine to five. Managers unload trucks at food banks, proofreaders clean up creeks, and accountants read to the blind. Whether or not volunteering is a way to make inroads into a new field, it is a direct and powerful way to express your practical idealism.

Practical Features of the Employment Landscape

So far in this chapter, we've mapped out a basic topography of employment sectors and discussed how to explore different fields. Now it's time to examine some specific features that shape your job landscape. This list of practical aspects, which was assembled on the basis of our own experiences as well as our interviews, includes schedule, travel, organizational structure and ethos, boss, and coworkers. We realize that not all of these questions can be answered thoroughly before starting a job. Nevertheless, we strongly recommend doing your best to get an accurate survey of your job prior to accepting a position.

Schedule

When our practical idealists assessed their jobs, an out-of-balance work schedule was the job strain most frequently cited. A few told us that the demands of their jobs made it hard to have a well-rounded life outside of work, while still others reported feeling that their work was so much a part of their identity that it was a real challenge to separate work and personal life. This isn't an issue that's singular to practical idealists, but it can be particularly difficult to untangle work and personal time when you've worked hard to find a job that represents who you are and enables you to live out your values. To be clear, some of our practical idealists did not appear to need this separation. On the weekends, some of those interviewed, for example, volunteered on direct service projects that addressed the same issues that they worked on during the workweek. While, as Noah Merrill pointed out, it's rarely a choice between ending a civil war and your family, your schedule does set parameters for your social life. If you're single and would like to eventually have a partner, for example, your schedule can mean that you don't have a lot of time to meet new people or cultivate a relationship.

While finding out the stated schedule of a job is a starting point, we all know that job descriptions aren't always accurate. Look at the job's duties to see if you think the job can be done within those hours. If possible, speak with others in the organization who have similar responsibilities or to the person who held the position prior to you. If you're working at a new organization or on a new project, it's quite possible that no one quite has a handle on just how much time certain tasks will take. If you've taken on a job or an assignment that requires a lot more time than expected, you need to let your manager or project organizer know. Otherwise they will never be able to create accurate estimates. Of course, if you're ignored and unreasonable timelines continue to be generated or if you're the one in charge and *you* continually, perhaps out of optimism or obstinacy, underestimate how long tasks will take, then you may need to re-evaluate whether this is the job for you or your self-management practices.

Practical idealists also need to look at the organization and see if it's one where the work ethos includes the expectation that people will work until they burn out. Jennifer Jordan, the research analyst for the Service Employees International Union, mentioned that she likes her job, but that people working as union organizers often have a tough time: "It's really intense. The understanding is, if you can't cut it you can't cut it, or you don't care enough to be able to cut it. And how do you complain about a sixty- or seventy-hour workweek when the people you're working for are working so many hours?" Other questions you may want to ask include, "How hard is it to take vacation time?" and "What is the policy on taking personal leave to cope with a family emergency or childcare problem?"

Travel

Closely related to the question of schedule is the question of travel. What are the opportunities for job travel and do they match up with your life needs? Travel may be a basic requirement of your job or merely supplemental, such as occasional conference trips. For some of our practical idealists, travel is a must-have with any job and for others it is mostly an onerous obligation. Practical idealist Jeff Isen was offered a very attractive position with ACCION International. Jeff, who has a masters in international relations, was asked to help expand ACCION's microfinance program in Africa through intensive training of African counterparts. This was a stimulating, hard-to-get job in his field—an almost perfect match with what he had thought he wanted to do. The job, however, required 40 to 50% travel, mostly with long trips to Africa to do the training. After much soul searching and discussions with his wife, Ana, who was just pregnant with their first child, he decided against taking the job. He also determined that an international career involving so much travel would never be a priority for him. He turned to another passion—being a high school teacher.

Some of those interviewed also pointed out that, depending on where you work, the actual mechanisms of travel can be tedious and time-consuming. Some larger institutions may have complicated reimbursement procedures while smaller organizations may lack a travel department and ask that you make all your travel arrangements yourself or that you pay everything out of pocket for eventual reimbursement.

On the other hand, your job may require too little travel for your taste. If you want to travel and the job you're considering doesn't already have opportunities for travel, are there ways to put travel into the job? Do funds for travel exist and will your job allow you time to be away from regular duties for job-related travel? You might also consider what sort of travel plans you can make outside of your job. Christiana Russ is a medical resident in Boston who is interested in international health. In order to get the international experience that she wants, she has taken advantage of her breaks and an elective to travel abroad and work in medical clinics that need additional staff.

Organizational Structure and Ethos

Organizational structure and ethos are the next important bearings to take when getting the lay of the land of a new or potential job. How large is your organization in terms of staff and funding? How hierarchical are its leadership and decision-making processes? Are the suggestions and ideas of staff taken seriously? Jeff Deutsch, graphic designer at Oxfam America, explains, for example: "I think at a place like Oxfam, and I imagine probably at a lot of other NGOs, there is a sense of democracy and a sense that everybody's opinion matters about everything." While this would generally be understood to be a good thing organizationally, as Jeff told Alissa, too much democracy and input, say in a design approval process, can make it difficult to complete projects in a timely fashion.

Another question related to organizational structure is whether or not the organization promotes from within and how it responds to people taking initiative. Knowledge of the way initiative is perceived in your organization and/or with your team or boss is as essential as learning if the organization generally promotes from within. When Alissa was an AmeriCorps member at the Peace Learning Center, a few positions opened up in the organization. Some of her fellow members applied for the positions and got the jobs. The organization also appreciated members taking initiative to conceive of or develop new programs and/or clients. Not all organizations promote from within, however. In many nonprofits and multinational organizations, for example, people fresh out of college can only get jobs as program or administrative assistants. These positions are often not direct stepping stones to program officer jobs. In many cases program assistants will need to go to graduate school or get experience at another organization before they can have a program officer or upper-level job. Alissa saw this dynamic at both the United Nations and the Carter Center.

Ethos, as we are defining it, relates to an organization's vision for addressing social change. Organizations are similar to individuals in that they run the gamut from liberal to conservative, radical right to progressive left. If your own politics and ideas about change fall near one end or the other of this spectrum, consider carefully whether you'll be happy at an organization that registers somewhere else on the scale. For example, many organizations work on international development issues, but their approaches vary widely. Some work more on increasing the participation and abilities of those being served, while others may be more focused on delivering services. Oxfam America, for example, has long been known for supporting the development goals of local communities. These goals are generally political as well as economic. There are other development organizations that see their work as providing services to people in need and ignore the political realm.

The internet, magazines, newspapers, and journals are all resources for learning more about a company's ethos and politics. Online databases like Lexis-Nexis, available at libraries, archive not only news articles but also company press releases posted to PR Newswire and similar resources. You can even find out if your company or nonprofit shows up in recent congressional hearing testimony (not always a good thing). You also need to ask people in your field, mentors, and professors what they've heard about the organization—taking care, of course, not to rely overly much on hearsay.

Boss

One thing about Nicole Hoagland's interview that struck Alissa was how excited she was when she spoke about jobs where she had a great boss and how disappointed she sounded when she described jobs where her boss was less supportive. Good bosses can help you understand your work and be more effective. They can also introduce you to others in your field and just be a good presence on the job. While job applicants often Google their interviewers or potential bosses, some important questions won't be answered in a web search. Are they good managers of people? Do they understand what it takes to implement what they ask you to do? What is their policy on asking you to do work outside the "normal" workday? Will they call you to ask for things in nonemergency situations and do you agree on the definition of a work emergency? Will there be good mentorship opportunities? Is your potential boss "old-school" or cutting-edge? In order to find answers, you can of course go to others who have worked at the organization, but often bosses have reputations that precede them and you might also talk to other people you trust in your field. Remember to be especially discreet and tactful during these conversations and never repeat, to anyone, anything that was shared with you in confidence.

No Job Is an Island

Before pursuing or accepting a position, consider whether or not your job will bring you into contact with ideas and people outside of your organization. Will you meet people from other organizations who are doing interesting work? Are there professional development opportunities like in-house training sessions or conferences and seminars? Is your business or nonprofit part of a broader network or coalition of complementary organizations that can help you with your work?

Several of the practical idealists we interviewed in the Research Triangle area of North Carolina, for example, met each other through a network of related organizations. These institutions actually had such a strong network that it became clear we had to conduct interviews in places outside the Triangle to get a fuller picture of some of the challenges facing those doing social change work in North Carolina. If opportunities to network with those doing work that is related to yours don't exist already, does your organization appear willing to let you create them?

Finding/Creating Practical Idealist Work

Flexibility and Stubbornness

After Alissa graduated from Amherst, she spent the better part of the summer miserable on her mother's couch. She was convinced that she didn't have enough experience for the jobs she saw advertised in her chosen field of international conflict resolution and she worried that she hadn't made sufficient networking contacts to find a job. She also knew that her student loans would be coming due in less than six months. What she discovered during those few painful weeks was that being a practical idealist requires a combination of flexibility and stubbornness. When conducting your job search, you too will have to find your own balance of these two qualities. This next section covers some keys to actually getting a practical idealist job, but the fundamental message we want to communicate is that you have to be both willing to try different routes to your employment goals (flexible) and tenaciously committed to the overall goal of expressing your values and passions through your work (stubborn).

Underpinning the flexibility shown by the practical idealists we interviewed is an understanding that there are a number of different paths to get to the same point and that progress is not necessarily linear. After some reflection, Alissa concluded, for example, that she could, as a first step, take an international job that didn't have a conflict resolution focus or accept a conflict resolution position in the United States. She was flexible enough to look for a job that focused on one of the subjects but stubborn enough to insist that one of those two elements be involved. Alissa's first job turned out to be as an AmeriCorps member teaching peace education and conflict resolution techniques in the Indianapolis school system. While she went the opposite direction on the geographical interest (deeper into the country rather than out of it), the position taught her skills she would go on to use in international work.

Another kind of flexibility shown by several of our practical idealists was a willingness to start out in a nonprestigious, entry-level position. Laural Horton, asylum attorney at Freedom House in Detroit, counsels: "Don't be afraid to take the lower-level, less glamorous job. Get your foot in the door; build the skills; do a great job at whatever you're doing and you're going to advance. Don't necessarily hold out for a certain title or a certain pay scale. If you go in, you are impassioned, you know what you're doing, and you do a good job at it, you are going to advance." John adds that, particularly at small nonprofits and offices, there can be a lot of mobility, because everyone tends to do everything. The director might help out with a last-minute mass mailing and the administrative assistant might take a crack at a response memo to a particular piece of legislation. John often tells students to work at a small organization first, get a good title in one or two years, and then move with that title to get a better job elsewhere.

As we mentioned above, Araceli Simeón Luna had an internship experience at MALDEF where her resourcefulness was appreciated. Later on, Araceli returned to MALDEF as an administrative assistant. She knew that the organization would not take her skills for granted and used her initiative to advance. She is now the National Parent School Partnership Director. "Once I finished my administrative duties, I would take on other projects that were needed....In nonprofit organizations there is a lot of turnover. Within the Community Education Department, typically people take it as a stepping stone into something else. [W]e get recent graduates, and after a year or two, they leave to go to graduate school or law school or better paying jobs....Within six months of starting as a secretary, I moved up to the trainer/facilitator position, working with the parents."

Remember Allison Greenwood Bajracharya, who reminded us not to be afraid to be humbled? She was talking about this issue exactly. Allison also said, "The prestige in a job description is not always satisfying, you know? If people are willing to say 'This is what I really want to do,' and do some crappy job for a while, I think it really pays off.

This is what I've seen. Don't be afraid to go out and take risks and do things that were not necessarily prescribed in a career path."

The major caveat here, however, is this kind of flexibility is only recommended if you're working at an organization that promotes from within and gives progressively more responsibility to those who have shown they can handle it. How can you tell if your workplace meets these criteria? One way is to check staff bios on their website. Are there a number of people who started out in lower positions than they have now? How long do people tend to stay there? You can also ask people within the organization and people in the field in general. If you decide to accept an internship, find out if interns are confined to photocopying or if they are given substantive work. Sometimes smaller offices are the best places to have an entry-level job, because the staff isn't large enough to be strongly segmented by task—so everyone has a shot at making a meaningful contribution. This is not always the case, however, and you've got to do your homework.

Foundations of a Successful Job Search

Doesn't it seem as though getting a job where you're helping people and working for social change should be easier to get than, say, a gig working for a tobacco company or weapons manufacturer? Well, it's not. The competition for some social change jobs can be dauntingly intense. The essential components for a successful job search, however, are not difficult to understand. In fact, you are probably already somewhat familiar with these three aspects of the job hunt: broad knowledge about the field(s) in which you will be working, networking, and self-marketing. In this next section, we will give you the basics of a well-run job search with concrete examples from the experiences of our practical idealists.

Knowledge of your field

Gathering information about your field prior to job or informational interviews gives you the ability to discuss your subject area and sound good doing it. The elements each person needs to know about their field will be different; however, you should always be familiar with the skills, methodologies, and major questions within your field. Your understanding of your field's fundamentals makes you a stronger practical idealist. It also makes you attractive in the eyes of those you network with and those deciding whether to hire you.

You should know what journals, trade papers, or websites are touchstones within your work community. One practical idealist who wanted to gain some Hill experience made certain that prior to her interview she read *Roll Call* and *The Hill*, as well as scanned local and national publications for news about the senator for whom she hoped to work. As she knew that she only wanted to work on the Senate side, she also made certain she had a good understanding of Senate procedure and an articulate reason as to why she preferred working in the Senate instead of the House.

Remember you may not always get your information and skills through previous jobs in your field or in the classroom. A skill is a skill and in the Dana Harrison school of thought, where a music teacher becomes the executive director of a social service nonprofit, what is important is that you have a skill and can use it well. If you get it through volunteer/unpaid work, jobs in other sectors, or a leisure time activity, you still have the skill. Knowledge can also be built in different ways. You might have a degree in your field, but, if not, a disciplined program of research, which would include taking advantage of any guest speakers who come to your area, can be productive and instructive. As you read this, there are thousands of college students who are not reading assigned material and planning on skipping class tomorrow. You can often find their reading lists online and their reading materials in a library or on the web. There is no reason you can't take advantage of their education.

Networking

Diane Standaert, a fellow at the UNC Chapel Hill Center for Civil Rights, is one of the most outgoing, gregarious, and warm people Alissa knows. Thus, Alissa was taken by surprise when Diane announced one day that she hated networking. If you like talking to people, you've got an advantage when it comes to networking, but introverts can become master networkers, too. A large part of networking is really just talking to a new person who does a type of work you're interested in or who has knowledge relevant to your field, which may help you in your job search.

Who to call while networking? The easiest people to start with will be your friends and family. While talking to your friends may not be what you'd normally think of as "networking," they are in your network and might know or know of people who would be helpful to you. You won't know this until you ask. In the midst of talking to people about what she would do after graduation, Kelly Letzler, who is presently the manager of Just 'Cause Catering in Indianapolis, found out that her boyfriend had gone to school with the son of Jean Paison, an Indianapolis pastry chef and the founder of Second Helpings, the parent organization of Just 'Cause Catering. Her boyfriend's friend put Kelly in touch with his mother, Chef Paison. The position that Kelly took when she first joined Second Helpings was not open when she started talking to this woman. She spoke with her just to get information about options in the sector. You can say this was luck, but if Kelly hadn't told everyone she knew that she was looking for a job, luck wouldn't have been able to find her.

Professors are another group of people you might already know who can be helpful. They are often plugged into networks of people in their field who know about interesting opportunities or places to look for work. They might also have their own research assistant positions to fill. As a student, Eric Greitens worked in the former Yugoslavia and in Rwanda with a group of students led by Duke University professor Neil Boothby. This work helped him earn a Rhodes Scholarship and put him on course for a White House Fellowship.

Colleagues are another good networking resource. When Laura Hogshead worked at HUD in Washington, DC, she found that her colleagues were more than willing to talk to her about the ups and downs of having a career in the public sector. While colleagues may be easy to talk to due to their proximity, professional associations can also be useful. Find out what associations people in your profession are active in, how you can join them and how you can get involved in work that will allow you to meet people doing the kind of work that interests you. When it was time for Sanchia Patrick to find a new job, for example, she was able to use connections through her professional association. A woman who was on an association committee with Sanchia told her about a job that may or may not have been advertised.

This person was able to first inform Sanchia about the job and also put in a good word for her with the business.

Alumni from your college or university are still another pool of networking connections. Many times career centers will help you make contact with alumni working in the field that interests you. If that office isn't helpful, you can ask your professors which alumni they've heard of doing work in their field or just execute a crafty Google search. Remember that these people may feel a bond with you, but don't assume that you had the same experience at school that they had. Just let the school connection gently open any doors that it can and take cues from the alum about discussing your school days.

While talking to your friends, professors, colleagues, and other contacts, remember to ask if they know anyone else in your field of interest. Christiana Russ, a medical resident, has also seriously considered going into the ministry. While networking, Christiana found that people were very apt to say, "Oh, I have a friend you should talk to." Truthfully, sometimes these referrals will hit the mark, other times they won't. Christiana learned that there were very few individuals who shared her very specific set of interests and that insight and information had to be gleaned from a combination of sources. Each new person gives you a connection to other people. Ask each new acquaintance you meet, whether helpful or not, for the names of other people (or organizations) they would suggest you contact. Remember to ask for current contact information for the person or organization and to ask whether you can say that they suggested you contact them.

There will be occasions when you are attempting to extend your network and you don't have any link at all with the person you hope to contact. Even if you are feeling boundlessly confident, contacting the executive director of an organization or another "name" personage is not always the most fruitful approach. Try looking a little deeper. Did this person thank a program officer or researcher for their help in a publication or during a speech? Did you go on the website or read about the organization and see that there is someone doing the kind of work you're interested in? If so, he or she might be a better contact. This person may also be plugged into communities and have suggestions that the director does not. This is especially true if the person is closer to your age and might have suggestions that are appropriate to people just starting out. That said, don't back away from approaching the director of an organization, if the right opportunity presents itself. Many are quite open and willing to talk.

As always, do your homework ahead of time to ensure that you are well informed and that your brief meeting will yield an in-depth discussion rather than just rudimentary details. Our practical idealists suggested that you ask questions about what they think the most pressing needs are in the field or the best type of preparation for working in the field. One person Alissa did an information interview with recommended that she think of a project that she would love to do and call the people she thought would be helpful with the project for advice. The same goes for getting information while writing a paper while in school. If you don't already have a project or a paper lined up, you should start one. With all the information you'll be amassing from your network, you should be able to shape it into a form that others will also benefit from. Another option if you have found someone whose work you really admire is to invite them to come and speak to a community group, campus group, et cetera. And if you're not already affiliated with a group, this is a great time to join. After all, they will become part of your network and open up more information and possibilities.

You might be saying to yourself, "This all seems so nebulous. You call a bunch of people to talk about the field in general and you're not even asking for a job." Remember, however, that most jobs are not advertised and personal contacts are the most direct and reliable route to a new job. In 2004, for example, Alissa was writing a paper about why the United States ratified the Convention on the Elimination of Racial Discrimination and not the Convention on the Elimination of Discrimination Against Women. In the course of her research, she called someone who had helped to write the congressional testimony given by an important nonprofit on the subject of this treaty. Alissa was able to identify him because he had been thanked for his help at the beginning of the testimony. It turned out that no one had ever called him to speak about this work before and they had a great conversation. She hadn't even thought about it leading to work in the future, but two years later, when he was in a new position, he hired her as an international election observer. This position was not on the organization's website and there was no way she would have heard about it without that personal connection.

Self-marketing and communication

Remember Dana Harrison, the executive director of Dress for Success Indianapolis, who started out as a music teacher? Dana's present work and varied career means that she understands the need to market oneself with savvy. Dana emphasized the importance of communicating the transferability of your skills to a potential employer. The two self-marketing tools that she spoke about were traditional yet effective: resumes and employment agencies. These tools are always useful, but the latter can be especially helpful when you're just starting out and/or your experience might not exactly be in the field where you're trying to get a job. Dana has some good advice for people regardless of how they get connected with a specific job listing.

> I think that there are two different styles of hiring. There is one style of hiring where the employer is looking at your degree, your titles, and your places of employment....On the flip side, there are employers who hire based on a skill set, potential, personality, and possibility. I think that if you're trying to make a change, you're going to be most successful when you connect with the latter kind of employer. But even so, you have to really understand and be able to demonstrate what your skills are and what it is you bring to the table. It can't just be jargon and the cliché phrases and words that are on cover letters and resumes. You have to be prepared for your interview and lay your resume and cover letter out in a way that talks about very specific accomplishments that you've made using a skill that you have that is transferable. You have to help an employer see the connection. You can't expect a potential employer to connect the dots.

Humble yourself and actually read a book on resume writing. There are plenty to choose from at career centers or your local library. Show your resume to a career center and knowledgeable friends for comments. And, for Pete's sake, proofread. Do not rely on your word processor's spellchecker. It will not catch everything. One of our practical idealists knows a foreign affairs legislative assistant in the Senate who almost (almost) sent out a policy memo where *public* was missing the *l*. In another case, an assistant for the Democratic National Committee, who used his spellchecker but did not proofread, sent out a financial appeal to the "Mashantucket *Kumquat* Tribal Nation" (it was supposed to be "Mashantucket Pequot Tribal Nation"). He was relegated to copying and coffee after that.

Josh Dorfman, founder of Vivavi, suggests that people have a blog. "Everybody is their own brand. We are constantly marketing ourselves as our brand and I think that the internet creates possibilities to build your brand so that you become known for whatever it is you believe in." With people searching for topics on Google, if you can get your message out and create some buzz behind you, even in a small niche community, "you're going to connect with people who are either going to want to employ you, buy your product, or collaborate with you."

If you do create a blog or self-market in another creative way, however, make certain to be scrupulously professional. A blog that lists what you ate for lunch or your "current mood" will *not* be helpful. And, though we shouldn't need to say this, we are taking this opportunity to remind you to watch what you post on social networking sites and to remove any pictures of your glassy-eyed self hoisting a beer stein.

Long-shot Jobs

At twenty-three, Alissa's friend, Meehan, was the successful director of a nonprofit organization that combined her activism on LGBT issues and her love of bikes. Meehan believes you should "go for" long-shot jobs. She points out that while you might get a job that you're not totally qualified for at that moment, if you don't apply, someone with even fewer qualifications could get the job. Such a person might not even know (a) how unprepared he was and (b) what he needed to do to get up to speed. At least you'll know what to work on to do the job well.

Now keep it real. If you're just starting out, applying for a directorship that requires fifteen years of experience is just not going to work. However, if there is a job that you think you can do and you see parts of yourself reflected in what they want, don't let your not having the requisite amount or exact type of experience scare you off. Apply for the job and let *them* say no. It was only after Alissa started doing some information interviews with people in the field who said that they thought that she had good experience that she started to have some faith in herself. While interning at the UN, a manager told her that job announcements were a wish list but there was often some flexibility in who they would take if they saw potential.

CONCLUSION

> It is difficult to define what we are, but our works speak for us.
>
> —Octavio Paz

Practical idealists *work* for social change. Otherwise they would simply be idealists. We know a job search can seem like an epic task. We also know finding a practical idealist job is not easy. It requires patience and persistence, in addition to flexibility and stubbornness. Almost every practical idealist that we interviewed did not take a linear path to their work. They were willing to venture away from the standard charted course to find what they were looking for. As the poem says, "Not all those who wander are lost." Nevertheless, a job search is not *The Odyssey* and you're not Odysseus. It won't take you ten years to reach Ithaca. You do have to hoist anchor and set sail, however. Practical idealists do; they don't just think about it.

4. Personal Finances

> Understandably, I make less money than some of my friends who went into the private sector. But I told them what makes it worthwhile is that I love my job. I look forward to going into the office every day and I look forward to the work that I do. As much as I might be irritated while I'm doing it, ultimately I enjoy it. So I said, for me, that makes it worth it. It's not that I have to make a huge adjustment to my lifestyle for the salary. I grew up in a very typical middle-class family. My salary will support that. It's not as tough as it might appear.
>
> —Samantha Yu

Your financial health is where the rubber meets the road with respect to the question "How much is enough?" In chapter 1, we asked you to think about "How much is enough?" in terms of the lifestyle you want to have, but you also need to think about it in terms of the compensation offered by the work you want to do. Practical idealists have a wide range of salaries and resulting choices in terms of lifestyle. What matters is how much is enough for you and being informed and strategic about money and credit. Finances are one of the most fraught subjects in many people's lives, whether or not they're practical idealists. In this chapter, we're focusing on the three money matters that are of greatest concern to the practical idealists we've interviewed: student loans, credit card debt, and settling for less-than-idealist jobs. We'll also discuss affording kids and saving while living a life as a practical idealist. As in other chapters, we will ask you to assess your current financial health and plan for fiscal stability.

Today, many students graduate with a debt load so burdensome that it feels almost theoretical. Credit cards are then sometimes used to make ends meet. These situations can be so daunting that people just put off confronting them indefinitely. Moreover, practical idealists can be so focused on social change goals that personal money matters can wind up at the bottom of their to do lists. Alissa and John know, for example, a talented recent graduate from the Fletcher School who, because his new job was so time-consuming, neglected to open his mail for a month—even though he knew the six-month grace period for his student loans was nearly up. He also had not taken the time to calculate whether consolidating his loans was a good option. You may be even busier than our friend, but if you don't stop to make sure your financial future is secure, you will undoubtedly be compromising it.

Dealing with Your Finances

Practical idealists may not be driven by money, but they do need to be well-informed about money, credit, and debt. If you understand the financial basics, you expand the choices and the avenues open to you in both your personal and professional lives because awareness is the first step to financial security. Financial stability may also put you in a position to make work choices that you wouldn't be able to make if you were financially insecure. Marie Trigona, for example, writes for magazines and websites in the United States and works with a social action video collective in Argentina. Marie writes about social justice issues but considers the work she does with the video collective to be her primary social change work. When discussing the video collective she says, "We completely self-finance our projects. That grants us autonomy, meaning that we don't have to depend on anyone." Marie knows that grants and funding criteria can constrain choices, but, because she had another source of support, she did not have to make unwanted compromises. At the personal level, financial stability can allow you to put more energy into social change work, community, and leisure activities, instead of struggling to secure basic life necessities.

Whatever the shape of your financial past, you can deal with it. It might take a lot of work or help from people with more information, but today is not too late to start making your situation better. Please note that "not too late" does NOT mean "okay to put off until tomorrow"! You can't ignore your debt. Interest on your debts accrues every day. Tomorrow you will owe more money than you did today. Interest on savings also accrues each day. The money you could have made by just letting your money sit in a basic index fund or Roth IRA will not be yours. Choices matter. Right *now.*

Debt is an emotional issue, not just a financial one. When you are in debt, you may begin to question your integrity, your self-worth, even your own identity. The emotional nature of debt often leads to paralysis. You may be too embarrassed to seek help, too uncomfortable to let your parents, friends, or even partner know about the whole situation. If this is you, you need to move past this stage. You must confront your fears and tackle your debt head-on. Accept the challenge. Stop blaming yourself or pointing fingers at others. This type of behavior is not helpful. Write down your plan, your commitment to move forward, and then share your situation with a friend or a sympathetic parent to get moral support. Then, as soon as you have developed your plan, move on it! Talk to your lenders and notify them of your plan for getting out of debt.

Student Loans: College and Graduate School

Many students graduate with debt equivalent to a year's worth of salary (Stephen Burd, "How Much Is Too Much?" *Chronicle of Higher Education*, August 2003). Aspiring practical idealists often tell John that, while they are studying for careers that express their values, they are anxious about their ability to pay off student loans. Practical idealists who have graduated describe the stress of living the fiscally responsible lifestyle necessary to make timely loan payments when their friends have accepted much higher-paying jobs.

There are steps you can take before, during, and after college and/or graduate school to avoid, lessen, or erase the presence of student loans in your life. In this section, we'll talk to you about some of these steps. Many of them are common sense, but you'd be surprised how few people take them.

FINANCIAL AIKIDO: NEUTRALIZING THE STUDENT LOAN BATTLE

Minimize the loans in the first place

- Investigate the possibility of money from family and friends
- Look for scholarship opportunities EVERYWHERE
- Work at an educational institution while pursuing your degree to receive discounted tuition
- Work for a company that will help you pay for your degree

Get help paying back your loans

- Explore schools with loan forgiveness programs
- Apply for jobs that may provide help repaying your loans
- Look for programs that give you an education award in addition to your salary
- Negotiate a signing bonus to use towards your loans

Making payments

- Take advantage of good loan consolidation programs
- Pay more than your minimum payment each month

Minimizing Loans Initially

If you want to get a formal education and do what you love afterwards, you need to minimize the amount of loans you take out in the first place. In order to do this, start as early as possible in the education process. Escaping college or graduate school debt-free is not easy. Based on numbers from 2004, 60% of graduating students had borrowed an average of $30,000 to $40,000. In addition, a 2005 study showed a dramatic increase in hours worked by college and graduate school students with 21% working twenty to thirty hours a week and 9% working over thirty hours a week (National Center for Educational Statistics 2004 and 2005, respectively).

Many of us don't have families who could, even if they wanted to, pay for our educations in their entirety, especially for graduate school. So let's assume that you've saved all you can and you still need money to pay for school. There is really no magic solution for what to do next, but the first step is having a reasonably accurate figure of how much you need. This amount will vary depending on the type of school you go to (if you are interested in schools with very different tuitions and costs of living, make multiple budgets). Many financial aid offices offer generalized budgets that list average expenditures for tuition, fees, books, housing, and other basic expenses. Plan to live simply. Simple doesn't mean having ramen noodles as a staple of your diet but might mean having roommates, using the cheapest transportation available, and keeping a tight rein on the thermostat to avoid crushing utility bills.

Once you have determined your budget requirements, you need to find ways to minimize the amount of money you borrow in order to meet those needs.

- *Research, research, research.* Scholarships are not just for the super academically endowed. Many scholarships are given by social service organizations, businesses, and churches for things like good citizenship, athletic or musical talent, or even business acumen. Most of these are not well advertised. You need to dig and then dig some more. Don't be put off if your potential debt is $30,000 and some of the scholarships you're looking at are "only" $1,500 or $3,000. Alissa received a scholarship for graduate school that was about $3,000, and it helped her pay for a semester and a half's rent costs. It's better to take the time to apply now than adding years to your loan repayment schedule.
  - ◊ *Websites.* There are good websites with scholarship information for college and graduate school. You can start by taking a look at sites like CollegeAnswer.com (use it for its tools and information, but be forewarned that it is managed by loan giant Sallie Mae and remember to apply for federal direct loans before anything private). You can also check out the financial aid websites of the schools you're interested in, as well as other scholarship sources such as FastWeb, CollegeBoard, and ScholarshipCoach.com. Avoid sites that charge you to search for scholarships.
  - ◊ *Students and financial aid office.* Talk to the financial aid office and to current students. Ask them how the students they know have paid for school and about any other scholarships or fellowships they may know about. Often students will learn about funding opportunities when it's too late for them to apply but are willing to share the information with others.

(Also, ask about loan forgiveness programs, which may be of use in the future.)

  - ◊ *The Foundation Center.* The Foundation Center (www.foundationcenter.org) is a clearinghouse of information on grants. It has a database of more than 6,200 grants to individuals, many of which are for educational purposes. You can access this information for free if you go to a library that has a "cooperating collection." This may be the main library in your city or at your university. If there isn't a cooperating collection near you, gather all your personal information and spring for the money to access the online database for the month.

- *Be a squeaky wheel.* Once the school of your choice has admitted you, let them know that they are your first choice, but that you cannot go there without a better financial aid package. Be wary if they suggest taking out more loans. What you want are grants or scholarships—which you do not have to repay.
- *State schools.* Go to a state university and laugh all the way to the bank. In-state tuition can be an incredible value. If you want to attend a state school that is not in your state, make it your state. In many cases, you can establish residency by moving to the state, working there for a year, and paying taxes. If you're doing this for graduate school, your college degree or already active resume should give you some interesting options for work. Consider trying to get a job at the school, which may allow you to take some classes at a reduced cost even before starting your program.
- *Paid internships.* Many schools will give you credit for internships. If you go to a school that doesn't offer course credit for internships, find a professor who might be willing to do an independent study with you. Explain that you'd like to do most of your independent study by working at an organization and writing a paper about your experiences and what you've learned. Find an internship that is paid, and you will be getting credit for time that you are making money. In addition, you might consider AmeriCorps programs, some of which are open to current students. Depending on the program, it may or may not have a stipend, but it will have an education award to help you pay for your studies.

- *Special programs.* There are some programs that give you college credit for work experience. This is most often the case for people returning to school after a long hiatus. Some schools have special scholarships for returning students. For example, the Real Program at Tufts University provides scholarships for older students returning to college after dropping out at some earlier time. The Peace Corps has also joined with a number of universities that will provide credit for returning volunteers. You may need to apply for the program before you are a volunteer, however.
- *Advanced placement classes (undergrad).* Check to see whether any AP classes you've taken can count towards credit. If you've taken any community college classes while in high school, sometimes those can be counted as well.
- *Transfer option (undergrad).* One option is to attend a community college or state college for a year or two and transfer to an elite school. It will save you a year or two of very high tuition. Make sure that your grades are strong in those first years and you are both known by your professors and active in your practical idealism. These actions will make your application more competitive.

How Much Do You Need?—The Right Loan Amount

It will probably turn out that you will still need loans in order to attend college or graduate school. The only way you'll know how much to borrow is by understanding how much you need during school. If you haven't already done so, sit down and make that budget that we suggested earlier.

Rule 1: Do not borrow more than you need

Any money you borrow today will be paid back with interest tomorrow. Some people's tomorrows last ten to twenty years, so the goal is to borrow as little as possible. Whatever happens, do not borrow more than you need. Jeff, now a public school teacher in Boston, has also worked on international education issues in places like Sri Lanka and Egypt. When he took out loans for graduate school, he did not have a budget. He simply took out the maximum amount the bank would lend him. Big mistake. He borrowed too much and graduated from college with loan money still in the bank. A little spending money to enjoy life might sound nice, but when Jeff spent the excess money, he got stuck paying back principal and interest on money he had not needed.

Rule 2: Go federal first
If you need to get student loans, apply for federal loans first. Stafford and Perkins are the two most common loan types. They have much lower interest rates than private loans. In addition, interest does not accrue while you are in school on the subsidized Stafford and Perkins loans and you get a six-month grace period after graduation before you have to start to pay back the loans, whether or not they are subsidized or unsubsidized. Simply put, they are generally the best deal out there. If you need to go beyond the federal loan programs, you can borrow from private sources, usually banks. Shop around for the best interest rates and terms. Remember to look at cooperative banks, like your local federal credit union. They may have slightly lower interest rates. Also consider the idea of a loan from a family member at no interest, or a low-interest loan that just keeps up with inflation.

Rule 3: Read the fine print (interest, fees, and payment schedule)
When Jeff graduated, the interest rate on his private loans was 5.5%. It jumped to 8.5% two years later. "At that point," Jeff says, "seventy-five percent of what I was paying the bank was interest." In the case of a (federal or private) loan that is not consolidated, your interest rate can rise with the interest rates set by the government. Those rates can change once a year and you need to know what they are. Other important details like fees and pay schedules will be covered under the section on consolidation below.

Keeping Loans Low Once You Start School
Once you make it to school, you'll have to remain financially vigilant. You will need money to live and to get ready for the next year of school bills. You have to keep looking for scholarships or better deals so that you don't fall into so much debt that you'll feel like you can't afford to pursue the career goals that brought you to school in the first place. Some of the strategies outlined above about scholarships and being the squeaky wheel remain relevant. You also need to pay attention to your lifestyle and the paid work you can do during school.

Working during school

There are both work-study and non–work-study jobs that you can take while you're a student. You may have received a work-study agreement as part of your financial aid package from the college or university you are attending. For John this was absolutely essential to making it financially. He worked as many hours as he could in the college dining hall. As he got more responsibility over the four years, his salary went up. You can also look for a job that will give you skills that will be helpful for your career or work with a professor who specializes in one of your areas of interest. Talk to the career office about different campus jobs that offer work-study. They may also know about off-campus jobs that offer work-study compensation.

Regardless of whether or not you are eligible for work-study, you can get a job. Depending on how hard you look and your previous work experience, you may be able to win a position that pays more than the work-study maximum. Many campus employment opportunities are work-study jobs only because the federal government helps your employer pay you, making you less expensive to hire. Some offices are more flexible than others about offering non–work-study jobs. Talk to people and get the word out that you're looking for work. Of course, how many hours you should spend on the job depends on your ability to juggle competing priorities and/or how much studying you can do on the job.

Student lifestyle

Student lifestyle used to mean ramen noodles, hot plates, and Goodwill chic. These days, credit cards and private student loans enable another world. But, take a look at the expense of living when you're paying tuition and not earning much income. If you're paying for your life with loans, each item you purchase will cost you a lot more than the initial price tag. Let's say you buy lunch for $8 and pay for it with student loan money. You may end up paying $12 for that meal depending on the interest rate on your loan and the amount of time it takes to pay it back.

As a practical idealist, you need to decide which expenses are crucial and which you can forgo for future peace of mind and a broader array of life options. In college and graduate school, lots of people seem to have money and live very well—eating out, taking trips, and subscribing to premium cable. It may not be easy for you to buck the trend, but it is probably necessary if you want to minimize your debt load. If there's a good bus system or you live near campus, you might not need a car, which comes with the cost of gas, car payments, and insurance. If you are a person who buys stuff that you know you don't need, practice the financial discipline that you will need to be a practical idealist. In graduate school with very limited money, John used to "live" at the library not just to study but also to take advantage of the heated room, saving on his fuel bill. We're not asking you to go that far; maybe you could just live with some roommates to split the bill. These are choices that you need to make to invest in your future.

Summer courses

At many schools, tuition for summer classes is less than for regular term courses. They are also often held in the evening, which would allow you to work during the day. Summer sessions may enable you to graduate faster and with a smaller bill.

Scholarships and the squeaky wheel redux

After you've gotten into school, remember it's not too late for scholarships and grants. Do more research on funding opportunities. Some opportunities may be created after you have started school or there may be things that you didn't find in an earlier search. Ask your classmates how they are financing their education and be sure to speak with graduating students who have had a few years to hear about opportunities. It's also important to reapply for scholarships that you did not get the first time but for which you are still eligible. Don't be afraid to politely seek out information on why you were rejected. While working on a graduate school admissions committee, Alissa learned that you can often find out why you were rejected, if you ask. The willingness to give feedback depends on the program. You won't know if the program that you're interested in will provide it, however, if you never ask. See if there is anything you can do to make your application stronger, such as pieces of your history or experiences that you should add.

Now What? Paying Back Your Student Loans

Saddled with $80,000 in student loan debt, a practical idealist said,

> I got into debt because I had no other means to pay for my education, internship, and living expenses while in graduate school. The feeling of having debt (for me) is something that constantly lurks over my head. There is a sense of shame and the feeling that I need to always explain why I have it, to reinforce the understanding that this isn't because I overspent on "wantful" items but that it was all for my education.

The day does come when you have to start paying off those student loans. You should have a strategy in place before that day arrives. You need a game plan for how you are going to pay the loans back *and* continue your dream of being a practical idealist. In the next pages, we will discuss three major options for managing your student loan debt: loan forgiveness, loan forbearance and deferral, and loan consolidation. Keep in mind that the latter two will not retire your debt, but they may be good options for ensuring that you can make your payments on time.

Loan forgiveness: Wiping out some of your debt

- *Your school.* Your college or university may have a program to help you pay back your student loan if you take a practical idealist job. Jeff had loans from his MA at the Fletcher School. A year after he graduated, he qualified for a $3,000 debt-forgiveness grant from Fletcher, and he can reapply for a grant every year. These programs are generally tied to your income and perhaps the cost of living in your city. They are also often geared towards people working in the nonprofit or public sectors. A growing number of public and private colleges and universities have similar programs especially for those receiving graduate and professional degrees.
- *Your job.* Some government agencies have small pools of funding to help pay off your loans. If you work for the public sector, check out whether you qualify for any. Public schools are part of the

Teachers Loan Forgiveness program. For example, Jeff, who is now a public school teacher in Boston, will qualify for $5,000 in debt forgiveness of federal loans after he has been teaching for five years. If he were teaching math or science, the amount would jump to $17,000. The National Health Service Corps program may pay $25,000 or more depending on the amount of time that a doctor or nurse has agreed to serve in an area of need. The business or corporation that hires you will not pay off your loan, but it may give you a bonus that you can then put towards your loan. When you are negotiating with your employer, see if a signing bonus or a special one-time bonus after the first year is an option.

- *Peace Corps*. If you have a Perkins loan, the equivalent of 15% of the loan will be cancelled each year during your first two years in the Peace Corps. If you extend your term of service, the equivalent of 20% of your loan will be cancelled each year during your third and fourth years. This means that if you complete four years of service, 70% of your Perkins loan will be cancelled. When you leave the Peace Corps, you also receive a $6,000 transition allowance. (These numbers were accurate at the time of publication, but visit www.peacecorps.gov for details.)
- *AmeriCorps*. The Corporation for National Service, which is the parent body that runs AmeriCorps, provides an education award of $4,725 to volunteers after each full-time term of service. A full-time term of service is 1,700 hours, which takes approximately ten to twelve months. There are some part-time opportunities, for which the education award is pro-rated. (Details available at www.americorps.gov.)

Student loan deferment and forbearance

Federal government loans, including Stafford and PLUS loans, can be put in deferment. If a loan is in deferment, your loan payments are postponed. Subsidized loans will *not* accrue interest, but unsubsidized loans will accrue interest that you will have to pay later or while in deferment. Most loan deferments are legal entitlements, if you meet certain criteria. Criteria include being at least a half-time student, a medical intern or resident, a full-time teacher in a designated shortage area, a member of the U.S. Armed Forces, or a Peace Corps or AmeriCorps

VISTA volunteer. Financial hardship, unemployment, and disability may also qualify you for loan deferment. Some private loan companies have programs similar to deferment so it is always a good idea to check whether you are eligible for deferment or a similar program.

If you do not meet the criteria for deferment, you may be able to postpone repayment through loan forbearance. Forbearance is granted at the discretion of the lender. In forbearance, *both* subsidized and unsubsidized loans will continue to accrue interest that will need to get paid at some point. In addition to financial hardship, there are community service programs that qualify you for postponement of federal and often private loans. Service in AmeriCorps, for example, which currently includes Teach For America, generally qualifies volunteers for forbearance. AmeriCorps also pays the interest accrued during service, provided the volunteer completes his or her term of service.

The rules on delaying loan repayment can change and different rules govern private and federal loans. It's smart to befriend a good financial aid counselor at your school or your loan holder. Also be aware that loans generally need to be in good standing (i.e., not in default) to qualify for deferment or forbearance, and loan consolidation can affect your ability to apply for either status. Some important questions to ask yourself as you consider delaying your loan repayments are:

- Do you really need to postpone your loan payments? Even if you postpone them, can you pay anything at all?
- What are your responsibilities, including financial responsibilities, during and after deferment and/or forbearance?
- What is the application process for delaying payment of your loans? What supporting documentation is needed?

Loan consolidation

Whether or not you benefit from loan forgiveness or delayed repayment, you will probably want to think about consolidating your loans. Consolidating your loans allows you to lock in an interest rate. This means if you consolidate your loans when the interest rate is low, the interest rate on your loan will not rise when interest rates go up. Conversely, if you consolidate your loans when interest rates are high, you will not benefit if they fall. In addition, if you consolidate all of your loans, your payments to various lenders will be merged into one single monthly payment.

Debt consolidation is a good idea for some, but it is not without its dangers. A good rule of thumb to remember is that it is rarely a good idea to borrow money to pay your debt. Loan consolidation is precisely that. The operating costs of many loan consolidation companies are funded by large banks and credit card companies, and the consolidator will be looking out for their interests, not yours. There are more aspects to loan consolidation than we can cover here, but, above all else, you must make sure to read the fine print of any offers you're considering. A place to start becoming educated about the consolidation process is the federal government's Direct Loan home page (www.ed.gov/DirectLoan). At minimum these are the things you should know before agreeing to a consolidation plan.

1. *Reputation.* Is it a reputable organization? Check with your financial aid office, Better Business Bureau, and fellow students. Don't be lulled by the label "nonprofit"—just because the company claims to be nonprofit does not mean they are trustworthy. Ask if the consolidator is accredited by the Council of Accreditation. Verify that counselors are certified and find out who provides the certification.
2. *Interest.* What interest rates will you pay during and after the first year? Make sure the consolidation saves you money *over time*, not just initially.
3. *Monthly payments.* What is the minimum amount you will have to pay each month?
4. *Loan term and early repayment penalties.* How long does the consolidation company think it will take you to repay your loan (loan term)? Are there penalties for repaying your loan faster than their expected loan term? Consolidators usually lower your monthly payments but extend the term of the loan (often lengthening the repayment period from ten years to twenty-five). The longer the loan term, the more interest the company makes and the more you pay. For example, if you decide to consolidate, make sure there is no penalty for overpayment or early repayment of the loan. Alissa's loan consolidation halved her monthly payment but changed the loan period from ten to twenty-five years. After she figured out

how much more she would be paying over the long term, she began to pay ahead on her loan. Paying ahead makes sense if the interest you are paying on your loan is *higher* than what you could earn by putting the extra money into savings or some other reliable investment. For example, if your student loan is financed at 6.8% and you can only earn 5% on a short-term CD or in a savings account, you will save money by paying ahead on your loan.

5. *Special offers.* Does your interest rate go down after you have paid on time a set number of times consecutively? Do you get a reduced interest rate for using an automatic payment system (a set amount is transferred from your bank account each month to pay your bill)?
6. *Delayed repayment options.* What are your options for loan deferment or forbearance once your loan has been consolidated?

The loan consolidation industry is highly competitive and aggressive. Loan companies will keep sending you mail—some of it scarily "official" in appearance with phrases like "Final Notice" stamped on the envelope. Some will send you checks to cash if you sign up. Others make you feel that your loans will be overdue if you do not sign up immediately. Many of these companies have chosen names to make you think that they're affiliated with the federal government. Do not be cowed. Unless the letter is from the actual institution that holds your loans (usually the federal government initially), it's just a gimmick. Also, be very suspect of companies that offer you cash incentives to transfer your loans to them.

Recently, the seamy underside of private student loans and consolidation has garnered a lot of media attention as well as the interest of congressional investigators. There are plenty of sources to read about other people's mistakes as well as reputable websites and books to help keep you from making your own. At the end of this chapter, we have included a list of books, websites, and other media that Alissa and other practical idealists we interviewed found helpful. Before moving on to our next subject, however, we do want to mention two specific student loan solutions used by some of the practical idealists we interviewed: family consolidation programs and working overseas to gain tax benefits.

Family loan consolidation

Jeff, the public school teacher, was working at a nonprofit doing international development while saddled with high-interest student loans. He worked out a deal with his parents where they paid off his high-interest loan using their lower-interest line of credit. Jeff then paid the monthly installment of their low-interest loan. The interest he saved made it worth it financially, even though he lost the tax deduction for the interest paid on the educational loan.

We understand that this sort of arrangement is not possible for many, but nevertheless it is an option for some. Another point to consider: if your parents have investments in short-term CDs or T-bills, you may be able to match their rate of return. If you were paying the federal government or a bank 6.8% and you pay your parents 4%, you're saving almost three percentage points—which can really add up in the long term. Depending on your relationship with your parent or "angel," you may want to have this agreement in writing.

Work overseas

Salaries overseas are usually more than you need to live, if you live within your practical idealist lifestyle. Depending on the country and how long you're there, you may not have to pay taxes. You can take the money you *would* have paid in taxes and use it to pay off your loans. This strategy worked for John years ago. More recently, when Ana and Jeff worked for Catholic Relief Services in Sri Lanka, they were able to live on one salary and squirrel away the rest. This meant that they did not travel extensively in Asia and they did not eat out a lot. They had a deliberate plan for saving one of their salaries, because they knew they were returning to Boston and wanted to have the money for a down payment on a house.

Student Loans—A Review

Before you get to school, you need to ask, cajole, and be the "squeaky wheel" that gets the attention of those with means to help you. Minimize the loans that you take out. Once you cross the Rubicon and take out a loan, be sure it has the best terms possible. Once in school, live within your means. Find ways of cutting your expenses and get the highest paying job you can while in school. Once you graduate, seek out programs that will wipe out part of your debt.

CREDIT CARDS

After student loans, the biggest financial burden is often credit card debt. John's daughter Ana now teaches workshops on financial literacy for a living at ACCION USA. She was lucky to graduate from college with no student loans to pay off. Within a year of graduation, however, she had an experience that gives her real empathy with her current students. "I had no idea that I could get into trouble as quickly as I did. I just went shopping and paid the minimal amount due and all of a sudden I had reached the credit limit on my credit card. It was all I could do just to pay the interest on the debt I owed. I had to get a second job."

Problems with credit can start early. If this is your situation, please realize you're not alone and that this is a national problem. Credit card companies push cards on people as soon as they graduate from high school. Many colleges allow credit card companies to set up booths as early as freshmen orientation week. Some schools have even partnered with credit card companies to offer affinity cards. These cards are usually decorated with the school's picture or logo and give the school some revenue. Unfortunately, they don't generally give students any special benefits, like a lower interest rate. Even if you avoided a credit card in college, when you graduate, companies find you and start sending a steady stream of pre-approved credit card offers. John and Alissa recommend that you remove temptation and get on the "do not mail" and "do not call lists" so that you stop receiving these offers. To stop receiving solicitations from credit companies in the mail call 1-888-5OPT-OUT (1-888-567-8688). In order to opt out and stop receiving credit offers based on these lists you will have to provide your Social Security Number. Make sure you call from a secure line when placing this call. For more information contact the Federal Trade Commission (FTC) at www.consumer.gov/idtheft.

Credit is not all bad, of course. You need a solid credit history and a good credit rating to get favorable rates of interest for cars loans, mortgages, et cetera. So let's say that you've decided to open a credit card account to build this good credit history. Please remember that you can build a good credit rating with just *one* card that you always pay on time. In general, you are better off with one, or at most a very few, credit card. This will help ensure that you don't extend yourself too much in terms of debt and managing your payments. A missed payment on one card will get transmitted to your credit report and may have an impact on all of your cards. When your credit report contains a notation of a missed or late payment on one credit card, card companies can raise the interest on your other card(s), regardless of whether you ever made a late payment to your other accounts.

Staying Out of Trouble

You may think you don't need to hear more about credit cards. After all, the media is full of cautionary tales of credit woes. The mortgage crisis that began in 2007 is only one more example of our national tendency to spend what we don't have. In a country where the average household savings rate is a negative percentage, apparently many more people, practical idealists included, need to develop credit card savvy.

Cash

In this day and age, using cash may seem anachronistic, but cash can be useful in helping you understand how much you spend. When you withdraw $60 from an ATM, and at the end of the day you only have $5 left, you really know what you spent. A few signed receipts just don't have the same impact. A big exception to this method is withdrawing cash using your credit card (a cash advance). The interest rate you will owe on your cash advance will be much worse than the interest you pay on regular purchases. Cash from your credit cards (and this includes those little checks that they send you in the mail) is never a good idea. And please try to avoid ATM fees; they can really add up. Remember, a $2 fee for withdrawing $20 is like a 10% surcharge.

Debit cards

Debit cards work well for everyday purchases, especially if you find yourself using your credit card to avoid having to pay ATM fees or carry cash. Debit cards access money that is *already* in your account and do not impact your credit history.

Paying your credit card balance in full within a fixed period
You can use your credit card without incurring debt if you pay off your monthly bills in full. If that's not possible, at minimum, follow this rule: Do not buy anything that you cannot pay off within one year. If you don't pay for it in a year, the interest on the item can add 20% or more to the original cost of the item. Suppose after graduation you purchase $2,000 in furniture for your apartment. You place this purchase on your MasterCard and never use the card again. Each month you make the minimum payments. Two years later your partner moves into your apartment and within two years you have your first baby. Meanwhile you are still paying minimum payments on your credit card purchase. Your baby will be ten by the time you have paid back the furniture. By then you will have paid more than $6,000 for the furniture! It would take you fifteen years to pay off the original purchase if you only make minimum payments on the credit card. Keep track of your credit card spending and income to make sure that your debt can be retired within a set time frame.

Read the Small Print—The Devil Is in the Details
Using cash and debit cards and paying your credit card bill in full are great ways to stay out of debt, but what do you do if you don't have that much available cash or that much discipline? You arm yourself with even more information and make some choices. You need to know these strategies even if you are using the three tools above. It can help you maintain good credit habits and improve upon a strong financial foundation.

Interest rates—How they can trap you
Like the Sirens in Greek myth, credit card companies will attempt to lure you into dangerous fiscal waters by offering a 0% interest rate. Within six months or a year, however, they can raise your Annual Percentage Rate (APR) to 17% or even over 24%. A 24% APR means that for every dollar you borrow, you will have to pay twenty-four cents per dollar per year, if you don't pay off your bill. And the interest for the next billing cycle will be charged on the interest owed plus the original amount you borrowed. Debt plus compounded interest can

add up very quickly. You can get yourself into a situation where you are just paying interest and making no dent whatsoever in the principal you owe. This is especially true if you're only paying a low monthly minimum on your credit card. For example, if you are just paying the minimum payment due each month, it would take you over ten years to repay an original credit balance of $800 at an 18% APR. At this rate, you would have paid $815 in interest—more than the original value of the item purchased.

Balance	APR	Minimum due	Monthly payments	Interest you pay	Months to pay off
$800	18%	$20	$20	$815.49	131
$800	18%	$20	$50	$121.72	19
$800	18%	$20	$80	$73.30	11

Changing APR

In order to avoid having your money eaten by interest, read the fine print on credit card agreements. Credit cards are not created equally. The interest charged, or APR, is the interest rate you will pay if you carry over a balance, take a cash advance, or transfer a balance from another credit card. Keep in mind that one credit card can have multiple APRs. For example, your credit card could have one APR for cash advances and another for balances carried over each month. Within balances held over each month you could be charged one rate for a balance of between $1 and $500 and another, higher rate for balances above $500. A credit card may charge a penalty APR for a single late payment or a delayed APR for a future rate that might be applied. For example you might be enticed by an initial APR of 0% but a higher delayed APR might be applied at a future time. You must therefore *read* the contract of your credit card to make sure you know if multiple APR rates occur.

Fixed credit cards claim that the APR does not change over time. This simply is not true. A fixed APR may change at any time for any reason as long as the credit company contacts you in writing to notify you of the change within fifteen days. This is why it is important to always read and re-read the contracts that you are bombarded with by your credit card company.

Interest rates are sensitive

Once you have signed a contract, the laws protecting the credit card company allow them to change the terms and conditions without your written consent. For example, even if you are making your payments on time with one of your credit cards, your interest rate can change automatically if you are late on making payments elsewhere—such as on your car, mortgage, or other credit cards—or simply because your credit card company believes you have opened up too many new accounts recently or have taken on too much other debt.

"Hidden" fees

If you think interest rate issues are scary, take a look at fees charged for bounced or unsigned checks, payments made by phone, or for late payments. People may refer to them as "hidden" fees, but if you do something to merit one of these fees, the credit card company will make sure it is listed in plain sight on your bill. Fees and penalties are applied even if you are five minutes late in making your payment, and many credit companies make it easier to miss a payment by making bills due at 1:00 P.M. rather than at the close of business. Other additional charges may include application and annual fees, which can range from $10 to more than $50. You can save money if you understand the tricks of the trade and read the fine print. One place to start is the website of the US Federal Reserve (www.federalreserve.gov), which publishes a semi-annual report listing the interest rates, grace periods, and annual fees of the largest credit issuers in the country.

Monthly minimum payments—The wolf in sheep's clothing

With some cards, like American Express, you must pay the full amount every month, but with others, like Visa or MasterCard, you only have to pay a minimum balance due each month. Visa/MasterCard companies often require minimum payments as low as 2 to 4% of the total balance. Under pressure from Congress, mega-lenders like MBNA, Citibank, Capital One, and Bank of America have increased their monthly minimums. Others may follow suit, but not all have done so. Remember, the smaller your monthly payments, the more interest you will end up paying. If your minimum payment is 2% and your interest is 18%, you still have your original balance and 16% interest on that balance to pay off for the next billing cycle. If you are unaccustomed to paying the balance in full at the end of the month, it might make sense to shop around for a credit card that requires a higher monthly minimum payment.

Maintaining or Building Good Credit: Credit Score

In order to maintain or build back good credit, you need to understand your credit score. Your credit score is your financial resume. The better your credit score, the better rate of interest you will receive when purchasing just about anything—a house or a car, for example. A favorable credit score also makes you eligible for lower credit card rates as well. Credit scores range from 300 to 850. Your personal goal should be to have a credit score in the range of 720–750. When your score dips below the mid-600 range, you only qualify for "subprime" lending rates.

Your credit score is affected by five factors: payment history, amount you owe, length of your credit history, how much new credit you've taken on, and the types of credit you are using. The best way to improve your credit is to make payments on time. Thirty-five percent of your credit score is your payment history, which includes the number and severity of any late payments. The most efficient way to get back on track is to pay your bills on time. If you know that you are going to be late on a payment, contact the creditor *before* the payment is due. You will be surprised by how credit card companies will be willing to work with you in order to get their money from you. In addition to making your payments on time, begin to pay more than the minimum amount due so that you can shorten your repayment period and reduce the amount of money you'll pay in the long run.

The second most important factor influencing your credit score is the total amount of debt you owe. Thirty percent of your score is how well you manage the debt that you owe. You want to keep low balances on your credit cards to boost your credit score. You need to know the credit limit of each credit card and always keep the ratio between what you owe and the card's limit at 2:1. In other words, make sure that at any given time, you owe less than 50% of your card's limit. For example, if the credit limit on your VISA is $5,000, owe no more than $2,500 on that card. Any amount charged over $2,500 will begin to lower your credit score.

The other three issues that affect your credit score are less important (though not unimportant). These factors are the length of time that you have been using credit, the kinds of credit you have (credit cards, mortgages, car loans, et cetera), and finally the number of accounts that you have opened recently. The longer you have had credit, the higher your score will be. You can therefore inadvertently hurt your credit score when you open new credit cards and close old accounts. For example, if you consolidate three credit cards onto one account, there is a possibility that you are damaging your score. This is particularly true if you are closing your oldest account to receive a better interest rate on another. Your credit score rewards loyalty, as do credit card companies. Instead of closing your oldest account, you are better off calling your credit card company to tell them about an offer you are getting in the mail from another company to see if they will match it. Remember your credit history is not static. From one second to the next your credit score can change as the information in your report shifts. Usually the last thing you want to do is erase your credit history.

A way to maintain a positive credit score is to diversify your portfolio. You want to have a mix of both revolving and installment forms of credit. Successful management of different types of credit will increase your credit score.

	Revolving Credit	**Installment Credit**
Example	credit cards	car loans, student loans, mortgages
Amount	Your credit card has a credit limit—the maximum amount of money that you are allowed to "borrow" each month. If you use your credit card responsibly the credit limit may increase over time.	You borrow a fixed amount of money depending on the purpose of your loan.
Payments	You pay back the money that you borrow from the credit card company each month and are given the option to pay only a portion of the total that you owe	Each month you pay a fixed amount of money to repay your loan.

Table created by ACCION USA

Opening a lot of credit cards at the same time can hurt your score because credit companies assume that it is possible that you can't afford your new debt load. Remember, each time you enter a department store and open a new line of credit you are affecting your credit score. Similarly, every time you apply for a loan with a car dealership you are potentially opening a new line of credit. If you apply for a car loan and open a few department store credit cards within a short period of time, your credit score could drop because you are now, at least statistically, a greater credit risk.

Getting Back on Track

If you find yourself closing in on the limit on all of your credit cards and only being able to make minimum monthly payments or missing payment due dates, then you need to take action now. Make a list of all your creditors, balances, and interest rates. Look at your monthly income and expenses and decide how much you can commit to repaying your debt. Write down your monthly repayment plan. Contact your creditors and notify them of your monthly commitment to repay. Ensure that, if the creditor agrees to your commitment, they send you a printed copy of your plan. Do not agree to commence payments until they have sent you a written contract. Once you have entered into an agreement, stick to it. Remember that debt is emotional. This process may be hard to think about, but it is within your abilities to complete. You are not the first person to contact a creditor and having a credit problem does not make you a failure.

The best way to get back on track is to get rid of your debt, one credit card at a time. Choose the credit card with the worst interest rate to focus on paying back first. Keep making at least minimum payments on all of your cards but put extra money into paying off the card with the highest rate. Once you have made significant progress on your credit card debt, consider opening a secured credit card with your bank. Secured credit cards are "secured" by money that you put into the account. You determine the credit limit. If you deposit $500 into this account your credit limit will be $500. Secured credit cards are a great way to reestablish your credit because you have control of the limit and banks report these cards to the three credit reporting agencies. Remember: just as with any credit card, do not spend more than 50% of the limit.

The approaches above outline only the most basic of financial tactics. One of the silver linings of living in a nation full of people up to their ears in personal debt is that there is no shortage of materials out there to help you formulate financial strategies that will work for you. We encourage you to explore the books and other media listed in the resources section, but don't forget to search for your own sources of information, as well. New books are being published every day. Just be certain your book:

- presents specific facts—for example, the mechanics of lenders' loan formulas or the difference between an IRA and a Roth IRA;
- helps you take an inventory of your finances;
- explores some of the possible reasons behind your spending patterns, which will allow you to break bad habits; and
- gives you ideas for budgeting and how to think about budgets.

Improve Your Credit Score

- Pay bills on time—even if just the minimum balance.
- Contact creditors if you are going to be late with a payment and work out a payment schedule.
- Pay more than the minimum required.
- Never max out credit cards. Use only up to 50% of available credit.
- Correct mistakes on your credit report.

Maintain and Build Your New Rating

- Open a secured credit card that limits your spending.
- Use a debit card for most things.
- Use only half of the credit line available to you on each card.
- Use credit sparingly. Purchase an item only if you know you can pay it off in the first year.
- Pay on time!

Less-than-Idealist Jobs

Student loans and credit card debt are not unique to practical idealists. However, debt can quickly stymie a budding practical idealist. Debt is scary. Friends, parents, and university counselors will often advise taking the highest paying job possible so that you can pay off your loans and "get on with your life." But as the practical idealists in this book show, debt does not have to jeopardize your practical idealism. You can still live out your passion, but you need to be savvy, prudent, and careful on financial matters. The question still remains, however: "Is it okay to take a high salary job just for the money and then switch to my practical idealist work?"

It's a question that many of John's students and other emerging practical idealists ask. In our minds, there needn't be any shame in deferring your practical idealist job in order to take a well-paid position that allows you to pay off student loans or other debt more quickly. Your aim is to pay off your debt, quit that job, and move into what you really want to do. It is a feasible strategy; however, as Detroit asylum lawyer Laural Horton reminds us, "Some people can't quit their corporate jobs after ten years when they've paid off their loans. You just have to put your values in place to see what is really going to make you happy." Many people who start down this path end up getting so wedded to the lifestyle that making the switch to practical idealist jobs can be very, very difficult. While John was at Oxfam, for example, he heard from many attorneys who had started their careers in big law firms just to make money and take care of their law school debts. But in the intervening years, they had committed themselves to large mortgages and lifestyle expenditures. Adjusting to a smaller salary now, they felt, would be too wrenching for both themselves and their families. Sure, they could do pro bono work at times, but they were convinced they couldn't work full-time on social change work until they retired—and who knew when that would be?

Law professor James Forman, Jr., suggests that people should start out working in a job they are passionate about and then decide if they want to switch jobs to work for money for a while:

> If you don't experience a job that you're passionate about early on, you might not ever know what it can be. You don't know what it can feel like to have that. You never have that bar for yourself. You don't actually know until you're fifty, when you have a mid-life crisis, what you've been missing, and then,

> a lot of times, it's too late. Based on my experience, my big advice to all of my students is to start with the thing that you're passionate about and then you'll at least know what that feels like. Later on you can decide if you want to give some of that up for something else.

If you have decided to take a job for money, there are some steps you can take immediately to help make the eventual transition to full-time practical idealist work. Research the jobs you want to take after you pay for your student loans or other debt. Have a firm plan for loan or debt repayment so you'll know when you have met your goal and it is time to leave that position for your practical idealist job. You may take home a bigger salary, but you need to spend money as if you already had the smaller salary. This is the case for rent, transportation, social activities, clothes, gifts, and travel.

You may not be able to live your life exactly as if you had the smaller salary, but you can live as closely to that reality as possible. One way to do this is to nurture social ties beyond those to your work colleagues. These can be people already doing practical idealist work or just those working to keep their costs down as well. This may even help you make connections for a future job transition.

The reality is, however, that some of your colleagues and friends will have more money to spend on entertainment and other perks than you will. But you need not "keep up with the Joneses" in order to remain friends with them. You will just have to be creative in finding social activities that don't involve a lot of spending. At times this will mean being honest and objecting when someone (usually the guy who has had two $10 martinis and a pitcher of imported beer) suggests that the $80 bar tab be split equally when all you've had is one bottle of Rolling Rock and a Diet Coke.

Andrea Strimling, who has also done work on practical idealism, explains that there is nothing wrong with making money. "Money is important. It allows us to meet our basic needs, and much more. What is important is to be clear about one's priorities, to have a strong sense of purpose in life and to use money to achieve meaningful goals, not just for oneself and one's family, but for others as well. How we make money also matters. We should consider the impacts of our work on other people and on the environment. And, for those of us fortunate enough to earn more money than we need, we should think creatively and strategically about how our money can be used most effectively. The answer is not always giving money away. Investing money in ways that both make a positive difference in the world and make more money, such as renewable energy or micro-enterprise, is an important alternative." Choices matter and you have to think about those choices before you make them.

HAVING KIDS

> It did not make financial sense for us to have kids. Of course it really never makes sense, but it clearly would have made more sense later. I resisted having kids at first. I was more practical than Casey. It did not make sense in terms of money and our time.
>
> —Nate Hanson

> I was emotionally ready for kids. I had wanted to have a child for a long time. When we finally were living in the same city, I thought it was time to have kids. It seemed to me that it was not going to make much more sense later on. Of course once I got pregnant, we both said. "Oh shit, what are we going to do now?"
>
> —Casey Hanson

Children take an enormous amount of time, effort, and financial resources. Some partners decide that children are not for them, but many practical idealists want to have children at some point. The decision to have children, whether or not you're a practical idealist, is only the first of a lifetime of choices that confront parents. Casey Hanson is a doctor serving her community in rural Maine. Nate Hanson is a furniture maker who is currently a stay-at-home dad. For Nate and Casey, deliberations about when to have children became discussions about who would look after the baby once she arrived. When they started their family, Casey was completing her medical residency, and Nate, who had left a PhD program at MIT, was just getting started as a furniture maker. "It was clear I had to stop what I was doing for one year to take care of Lily," said Nate. "At first it was going to be one year only; but now we have had a second child, so really I have put off what I was doing for four years." When their eldest child, Lily, starts kindergarten, the money they now spend on pre-school for Lily will go towards part-time childcare for their younger son, Winslow. At that point, Nate will be free to restart his furniture making business.

Nate and Casey admit, though, that while these choices have worked for them, it has involved sacrifices. Casey feels the pressure of being the family's sole breadwinner, and Nate acknowledges that he will have to work to regain momentum and confidence in his craft. "[Before taking time off to care for Lily] I had just started my first commission piece. I was ready to make a go of it. So, I had to put on the brakes on my making furniture. It was not easy, but I was the one who had to do this. I sacrificed the momentum I had. It did not seem like that much of a sacrifice at the time. I now feel that I am getting rusty. It will take me some time to get back into making furniture."

As in all things practical idealist, choices matter. Even though Casey and Nate owed over a hundred thousand dollars in student loans and had some credit card debt, from Casey's medical school and residency period, respectively, they decided that they wanted to have children sooner rather than later. Nate and Casey are now on track for their goal of being able to retire early: "We will be 51 when our kids finish college. We want to retire, buy a boat, and travel on our boat."

Nate went on to say that,

> At this point the way we express our commitment to broader issues is by focusing on our local community. We are careful about where our food comes from. We support our local agriculture; we get all our meat and dairy from locals that we know within 20 miles of our house. When we are more settled financially we plan to expand our work for the local food shelter and the free clinic. In the long term, once the kids grow up, we have talked about being foster parents. We have also discussed sailing into the sunset on our boat and using our skills in other places. We both have skills that allow us to go anywhere.

Casey and Nate deliberately chose to raise their family in an area in Maine where housing and other costs were less than they would have been in Boston or another large city. Casey's job at the hospital allows her to work 80% time instead of full-time so she has more time to spend with her family. Casey says,

> We wanted to work where we did not have to work all the time. In our case, we moved to Maine. We wanted to work less and be able to pay off the cost of a house, a car. In the big cities, people work for money and they can never get ahead. The more you make, the more you spend. It seems like if you earn more then you justify spending more.

Many practical idealists consider raising children to be their most important work for social change. Jeff, for example, was very clear that being a good father was part of his practical idealism.

> I became a teacher of high school....If I had stayed in a corporate environment (nonprofit or private sector), they are always asking you to take on more responsibility, bigger and bigger jobs. This means that you sacrifice more and more of family time. I did not want to be an absentee father. For me an important part of being an idealist is being an active parent. I may not make a million bucks, but I will be a present father.

Practical idealists, like all parents, have to consider many strategies in order to make ends meet and support their families. Sometimes parents work full-time while their child is in daycare or looked after by a nanny or relative. Other options include having one partner work while the other remains at home or having one partner work a part-time or flex-time job and look after the kids when he or she isn't working. Ana, for example, has a flex-time position that allows her to take one day off a week. One of her neighbors, who also has an infant and a flex-time job, has agreed to watch Ana's baby along with her own on her day off and Ana will reciprocate on her day off. This arrangement will cut their childcare expenses by 40%.

Flex-time is only one of the family-friendly policies offered by Ana's employer, ACCION USA. When you're looking for a job, be sure to examine the family policies of your organization. Ana told us, "I found a job that encourages families, allows you to work flexible hours and has good family benefits. This has made it easier to think about having a kid." For Ana, it is more than just family benefits and time off. She says: "My career itself supports kids. I do trainings mostly for immigrants. They often bring their kids to the workshops; I will be able to do the same. This makes me feel that I can raise a kid and also perform well in my job."

Living and working in overseas locations, where the cost of living is lower and you may not owe US income tax, is another option that makes it easier to afford childcare or for one partner to stay at home in order to watch the kids. Jeff reminded us, however, that there can be drawbacks to this approach. "I pulled out of an international job in part because there was not a positive attitude abroad for raising kids. There was so much poverty and then a very wealthy elite. I worried about them growing up with values that I did not want them to have."

The choice of whether or not to have children is an intensely personal one, and what is intellectually "rational" or "practical" is not always the right decision. Practical idealism has nothing to say, really, one way or the other, about the wisdom of having children or even when you should have them. Once children arrive, however, the practical aspect of practical idealism comes to the fore. Practical idealists who have children may find it more of a challenge to find work that both expresses their practical idealism and allows them to be the kind of parents they hope to be. It's possible to have a happy family as a practical idealist, but it does involve sacrifice and careful stewardship of your resources, both financial and personal. But then again, being a parent has always been about making important, and often difficult, decisions.

Savings

We would like to conclude this chapter by talking about something Americans, as a rule, don't do much of: saving. If you're not already in the habit of saving, now is the time to start. Even if you can't save much, even if your organization doesn't offer a 401k or other retirement savings plan, you need to begin. Saving is not just about setting money aside for a rainy day or retirement; it's about finding ways to *not* spend money.

Ways to Save

Have you noticed that you spend less when you have less to spend? If you withdraw a large amount from the ATM, are you a freer spender when you're walking around with $100 in your pocket? Do you think that you should be able to save at least some money, but in reality you don't really have any savings? We recommend that you take some tried and true advice: When you get your paycheck, pay yourself first, however small that payment may be. You spend the whole month paying everybody else—your landlord, the transportation authorities, the burrito place down the street....Give yourself the same courtesy. Put some money directly into a savings account. (This should be in addition to your 401k or any other retirement plan you may be participating in.) Often a smaller checking account balance helps to put the brakes on discretionary spending. Just remember not to let your money languish in a savings account that only offers a low interest rate. Once you have accumulated a set amount (say, $500), move your money to a low- or no-risk investment where it will garner a higher rate of return.

During the interviews, many of our practical idealists shared the creative ways they had found to increase their savings:

- "Latch onto conspicuous consumers for their hand me downs." We all know people who need the latest "it"—whatever it is. "It" often includes adult clothes, baby clothes, toys, electronics, even cars. Benefiting from other people's purchases can happen on a one-on-one basis or in a group. Alissa has friends all over the country who host clothing swaps. This allows them to get rid of old stuff while finding new treasures.
- Think about living in a smaller city or rural area where housing is less expensive and the cost of living may be lower. Few people can afford to buy a home in cities like Boston or San Francisco, but if you live well away from a major metropolitan area, your rent or mortgage payments are likely to be substantially lower.

- Bartering isn't just a thing of the past. You may have a skill, service, or item that could be useful to someone who has something you want. See if you can make a trade. A graphic designer can trade a few hours of web design for two massages from a massage therapist working to open an independent practice. Many places, including yoga, art, and dance studios have official work-study programs where you trade your labor for free classes or space. Money isn't the only way to acquire something you want or need.
- There are many other ways to be creative in saving money. Eat out all the time? Comparison shop to see what restaurants have the best meals at the cheapest prices. Also assess whether the takeout portions are larger than the eat-in portions so you have leftovers for another meal. Have a latte habit? Go online, get a good deal on a machine and actually use it. Really need a gym membership? Check out the Ys in your area. Need cable just to get reception on your TV? Check to see if the shows you want are on the internet for free. Find yourself buying the same magazine as a guilty pleasure every month? Get a subscription and maybe even split it with a friend. Need to set up a house with pretty things? Go to a student art show, find something you like, and approach the student about buying it. You get the idea. Be creative and try something old in a new and cheaper way.

As you can see, there are many approaches to saving money. Some of them, like the ones in the last bullet point, may sound silly, but they work. If you find yourself unable to make large life changes, start small and force yourself to keep going. There are ways to spend less money while keeping what you feel you can't give up. In the end, there are some things that you may still have to do without, but you have choices. Saving money isn't about restrictions. It is about looking at how you actually spend your money, how you want to be spending your money, and making the choices that are necessary to make that change.

CONCLUSION

In this chapter, we have focused on the kinds of financial choices practical idealists encounter in their daily lives. In doing so, we have essentially taken the current economic system and its emphases as givens. We want to point out, however, that there are practical idealists who are challenging the economic status quo and the fundamental consumerist assumptions that underpin the current economic system. In her article "What Is the Economy For?" economist Neva Goodwin, co-director of the Global Development and Environmental Institute at Tufts University, argues, for example,

> [T]he reason we want jobs is to earn the income that will allow us to purchase the things we need and want. It is not easy to define precisely what constitutes adequate food, shelter, support for health, and care for the young, the old, and the infirm; but even without precise definitions, we can at least point to these as immutable needs. Wants, however, are another matter: they are highly suggestible, and the satisfaction of wants does not always lead to well-being.*

Whether or not a shift in consumer wants occurs on a national level, practical idealists know that their financial choices matter, both on a macro level and in their personal lives. How you cope with student loans and other sources of debt, as well as your spending and savings habits will, in large measure, determine how free you are to pursue your practical idealist calling.

Our economy is consumer dependent and that's what we all do—we consume. We are a nation of fast food and fast credit. And just like when we drink too much or eat too much, we know we'll regret financial overindulgence later, but we often close our eyes to the future consequences. Sooner or later, however, your health suffers, whether it's your physical or financial health. Bad consumption patterns in our diets lead to diseases like diabetes, which can damage our bodies and limit what we can do physically. Careless financial habits can injure you as well, restricting the breadth of your life choices. Making good decisions about your financial life is hard, otherwise everyone would be doing it and our nation wouldn't have a negative savings rate. However, financial discipline, like a life dedicated to practical idealism, becomes

---

*Goodwin, Neva. "What Is the Economy For?" *Opinión Sur*. August 2007. http://ase.tufts.edu/gdae/Pubs/te/OpinionSur_NevaGoodwin_Aug07eng.pdf

easier with practice and experience. Remember that personal and social change are connected. As a practical idealist, you approach social issues with informed and strategic action. You must do the same thing with your finances.

The Mañana Trap

- Deal with your finances *now.* If you sleepwalk through your financial life, sooner or later, you will wake up to a fiscal nightmare.

Assess and Shape Your Spending and Savings Habits

- Make sure you are spending money in ways you support. Being uninformed about your habits or rationalizing individual purchases can add up to debt very quickly. Make sure your "spending" includes paying off your debt.
- Get in the habit of setting aside some income as savings—even if it is only a small amount.
- Plan for the new additions that the future will bring and take the steps to be ready for them.

Financial Literacy Is Your Best Friend

- Become informed about your own finances *and* the larger financial systems that affect you. What you don't know really *can* hurt you.

RESOURCES

The following resources are not meant to be a systematic survey of materials or an endorsement of certain authors. They are simply resources that have been mentioned by the practical idealists we know. Check them out and see if there is something here that could work for you.

Fred Brock. *Live Well on Less Than You Think: The New York Times Guide to Achieving Your Financial Freedom*. New York: Times Books, 2004.

M.P. Dunleavey. *Money Can Buy Happiness: How to Spend to Get the Life You Want*. New York: Broadway Books, 2007.

Frontline, "The Secret History of the Credit Card" website: http://www.pbs.org/wgbh/pages/frontline/shows/credit/.

Anya Kamenetz. *Generation Debt: How Our Future Was Sold Out for Student Loans, Bad Jobs, No Benefits, and Tax Cuts for Rich Geezers—And How to Fight Back*. New York: Riverhead Trade Books, 2006.

Ken Kurson. *The Green Magazine Guide to Personal Finance: A No B.S. Money Book for Your Twenties and Thirties*. New York: Doubleday, 1998.

Suze Orman. *The 9 Steps to Financial Freedom*. New York: Crown Publishers, 1997.

Suze Orman. *The Money Book for the Young, Fabulous and Broke*. New York: Riverhead Books, 2005.

Sarah Young Fisher and Susan Shelly. *The Complete Idiot's Guide to Personal Finance in Your 20s and 30s*. Upper Saddle River, NJ: Prentice Hall, 1999.

Elizabeth Warren and Amelia Warren Tyagi. *All Your Worth: The Ultimate Lifetime Money Plan*. New York: Free Press, 2005.

5. Community

Araceli Simeón Luna's parents hoped that she would get a job working with computers; Samantha Yu's family was skeptical of her decision to work in government; Jeff Deutsch found that new acquaintances assumed that he disapproved of their corporate jobs; Sarah Haller's dad worried that she did not have a career path. If your parents worry that you'll wind up homeless or living in their basement indefinitely, your friends wonder if you're judging them for making more money, and it feels as if the rest of the world is shaking its head at your naiveté...relax. This is not unusual.

As a practical idealist, you will be pushing to do something that is innovative, creative, and different from the path that most people follow. It is possible that even those who were traditionally your most stalwart backers may find it difficult to summon their usual enthusiasm with respect to your choices. Worse, the more idealistic you are, the more you will attract naysayers. Even casual acquaintances may seem compelled to inform you that your idealism is impractical and possibly even irresponsible. In addition to the uncertainties and challenges present in any career, practical idealists often cope with being dismissed as quixotic while at the same time wrestling with the question, "Am I really making a difference?" In order to survive as a practical idealist, you need a support system; you need community.

Every practical idealist we interviewed affirmed the importance of having a community of support in place. This community is often, as Carmen Patrick Mohan referred to it, a "cut and paste" network of parents, family, partners, friends, mentors, neighbors, professional associations, and faith groups. Just as no person is any one thing, a community of support is also made of many parts. Some in your community will offer unqualified and total support; they are the ones who cheer you on unreservedly as you try to change your corner of the world and live out your passions and values. This "back-up choir" urges you on when you become dispirited and reminds you that you have unique talents to offer the world. As a practical idealist, however, you also need advocates who have the practical knowledge and skills to aid you in reaching your goals. These practical mentors and advisors will help you make your idealism practical and allow you to survive and thrive over time. Your community of support also plays a role in your self-examination and assessment process, providing you with essential feedback. As corporate product manager and nonprofit founder Sanchia Patrick explained, "You need a circle of people to hold you accountable—not just your colleagues."

Sustaining and growing personal community is foundational to a life of practical idealism. Those interviewed for our project all relied on a combination of family, friends, mentors, and other networks for emotional, intellectual, professional, financial, and spiritual support. The link between individual transformation and social change, a fundamental premise of practical idealism, works both ways: you work to change and improve your community and your community helps you to transform and grow. In the remainder of this chapter, we examine examples of social support and resistance in the lives of our practical idealists and explore the different groups that together create constructive community.

A la Familia: Your Family and Your Idealism

A quick glance at the "self-help" section of any bookstore will reveal a daunting number of books devoted to untangling knotted family ties. The relationships practical idealists have with their parents and siblings are no more or less fraught than other people's, but practical idealists can sometimes face unusual hurdles in communicating the reasons for their life decisions to their families. While our interviewees reported various levels of family support or nonsupport (both moral and financial), nearly all of them had to, at some point, try to explain their practical idealism to their community of family.

Some of our practical idealists had a relatively easy time declaring their need to follow a nontraditional path. The parents of Josh Dorfman, the founder and director of eco-design firm Vivavi, were themselves entrepreneurs who ran a sleep-away camp in New Hampshire. Although Josh had steered a nonlinear course prior to starting his company, a path that included ski bumming in Colorado, an extended stint working in China, an attempt at screenwriting in Los Angeles, and a brief career in eBay arbitrage, his parents remained supportive. As small business owners themselves, they even helped to vet his business plan for Vivavi. Grassroots environmental organizer Annie Sartor found that her father, whose moral outrage at the Nixon Administration's illegal bombing of Cambodia had fueled his decision to work in Ethiopia for the Peace Corps in the early seventies, understood her own desire to work for a better world at Oceana, an organization that focuses on protecting the Earth's oceans.

On the other hand, the terrain of practical idealism is terra incognita for many parents and guardians. Several of our practical idealists admitted that their parents were concerned about their unconventional career choices, disagreed with their politics, worried about low earnings, or just found their child's undertakings on behalf of social change baffling. Nicole Hoagland put it this way: "Mom was an activist in her early years, but I think that my being in a small, gay organization in North Carolina is a bit too much for her." During a visit home, union analyst Jennifer Jordan found friends and family held negative perceptions about the labor movement, believing that union rhetoric "was a bunch of union fat cat talk and labor unions hadn't ever done anything for black people." Prior to landing a job at the Service Employees International Union, Jennifer also found that her job search was "one of the first places I had a huge disconnect with my mom. I think that her understanding of a job is that a job is what pays you. You're lucky if you like it." Jennifer wanted a job that did more than just pay the bills.

Of course, parents being parents, confusion or even disagreement does not necessarily preclude them from offering support. Kristen DeRemer's life has taken her to Thailand, Uzbekistan, Rwanda, and Northern Uganda—seemingly light years from the rural town where her mom is a schoolteacher: "It took my mom a while to get used to, but she has always just been incredibly supportive." Older members of David Neal's family were "avid supporters of the death penalty," but this did not prevent them from continuing to offer love and support when he started the Fair Trial Initiative, an anti–death penalty organization. Although still in favor of capital punishment, after talking with David, his relatives were able to understand that his involvement with the Fair Trial Initiative came from his desire to see the law applied more fairly and equitably—a value that they shared.

Whether or not your parents and family agree with your life choices or the particular issue you may have chosen to champion, remember: you are not gay rights, world hunger, or the death penalty. You are a daughter or son or sister or brother, and your parents and relations do not have to accept your position on any particular issue in order to be supportive of you. It is possible to receive support from your family community even if they do not agree with all of your principles or even fully understand your practical idealism.

After encouraging you to follow your passions and values in previous chapters, it may seem counterintuitive for us to separate emotional from intellectual support, but mature relationships must sometimes reconcile a fierce devotion to a cause with the devoted support of those who disagree with you. As Noah Merrill, Quaker organizer and co-founder of the Iraqi refugee assistance program Direct Aid Initiative, explained, "Just because I suddenly got religion, in the sense of understanding a particular social issue or dynamic, doesn't mean [my family is] suddenly evil because they don't understand it too."

Conversations with parents and other family members are often not very easy, but if your family is to be part of your community of support then they have to happen. Noah Merrill cautions against avoiding these sometimes difficult conversations:

> I guess what I have learned in terms of the mistakes I've made is that I was afraid to engage and because of that I ended up nearly permanently severing some relationships. And in fact, the suffering and the pain of not having those relationships is far worse than the suffering and the pain of having them have to accept me as an adult. They don't have to approve of

everything I do, but they actually approve of a lot more than I thought they would.

In both David and Noah's cases they were able to talk openly about their practical idealism and their chosen issues. In David's example, while some members of his family did not agree with him, they were able to see the merit in his passion for equity in the criminal justice system. If you feel like your family might be experiencing some doubts about your practical idealism, consider asking them the questions on the list below so you can better understand their position and they yours. You might not want to take the time to have your family answer these questions, but you can be certain that, unless you are completely divorced from your family, you will learn the answers to these questions sooner or later, whether indirectly or directly. Asking them in a direct manner means that the answers can come out in an environment of your choosing rather than during some uncomfortable moment over sweet potatoes at the Thanksgiving table.

One good way to start a conversation is to lay out what you plan to do and why. Be sure to explain not just what you will do, but also your particular passion and the importance of this path for you. They do not have to agree with you. The follow-up discussion might include asking your family questions similar to the ones on this list.

1. Are there things that scare you about me taking on this kind of work?
2. Are there things that excite you about me doing this kind of work?
3. If you are worried about my safety, is there anything I can do to assure you that I will be safe?
4. Do you see why I would want to do this, even though you think it is risky (or crazy or weird or naive)?
5. Do you have any suggestions for me about doing this kind of work? Are there questions I should be asking, skills you think I should develop, or people you think I ought to talk to?

Your family might not be thrilled about your practical idealist choices, but they can still be part of the process. Two years after graduating from college, Alissa was offered the opportunity to work with a human rights organization in Rwanda. When she told her mother about the job, she could hear concern in her mother's voice. The next day, an email from her mother with a list of questions was in Alissa's inbox. These were questions that her mother thought Alissa could ask in order to get a clear picture of the political situation, the organization's work, what she would be doing, and the risks involved. Alissa had already decided not to pursue the opportunity, but found the list so useful that she kept it to use for work decisions in the future.

Before talking with your parents or other family members, however, there are two questions that you should really ask yourself first:

1. How necessary is it for you to persuade family members of the justness of your cause or the appropriateness of your career choices?
2. Do you want them to understand or agree? There is a big difference between wanting to be understood and wanting to be right. And, if they cannot understand, will you be content if they agree to respect your choices?

There may be times, even after you've made the effort to explain and listen, that mutual understanding proves elusive. But, if the idea of never reaching a meeting of the minds over your career choices depresses you, remember that sometimes opportunities for a little bit more clarity or understanding sneak into your relationship at unexpected moments. Nicole Hoagland, for example, told Alissa this story: "My father sat down with me many months ago and said, 'You need to think about retirement and money.... You're not making any money....'" At the same time, Nicole's mother came over with an article from the local newspaper about a young man who had been helped by Nicole's organization, Time Out Youth. As a young gay man growing up in the South, he felt isolated and had twice tried to commit suicide. Time Out Youth had given him a place of support and a community of friends. "He had just blossomed into this incredibly compassionate, capable individual living in this world." She told her father, "Not for a million dollars would I change the feeling that I just got from reading that article." Nicole continued, "There is no money that's worth that. There's just not."

Parents and family can be allies, neutral parties, or even, at times, opponents to your practical idealism. Whichever of these best describes your own situation, if your family is part of your community of support, then discussing your life choices will happen—one way or another. If you are able to enter into a conversation in a prepared, kind, and nonjudgmental fashion, then it is possible that your family will discover how to better support you in your practical idealism.

IN THIS TOGETHER: A COMMUNITY OF TWO

At the end of the day who you come home to is more important to your practical idealism than those work colleagues that you left behind at five (or six, or seven) o'clock. For our practical idealists with partners, those partners form the most basic unit of their community. Unsurprisingly, our interviews showed that this "community of two" shapes and influences your practical idealism and your practical idealism in turn affects your relationship. Carmen Patrick Mohan, who lives a demanding life as a physician, healthcare advocacy nonprofit co-founder, and activist, referred to her husband as a "huge, renewable kind of replenishing energy." His support sustained her and her practical idealism. Mel Rodis, likewise, needed her partner's financial and emotional support in order to pursue her dream of becoming a "working-class" lawyer: "I'm just in pro bono cases right now. So I have no income. I'm in a tremendously privileged position to be able to do that because of her love and support and her belief in me and in giving me a break—because I am sort of in a transition period. It's allowed me a lot of time for self reflection but also to take on the kind of stuff that I care about."

John was married to his wife Tina, a teacher, for over thirty-five years—a partnership that allowed him to raise two active daughters while executive director of the nonprofit ACCION and later of Oxfam America. While he originally worried that having a wife and kids would compromise his ability to work for social justice, he "found over time that marriage was not in fact, limiting, but rather liberating. By having a solid relationship grounded in love, we were able to move out of that relationship into meaningful work in society. My wife kept me honest and kept me focused. She kept reminding me that life was not all ideology and social action and public advocacy. Effective work flowed from good personal relationships, from loving relationships."

The mantra of practical idealism is "choices matter" and, if you are in a committed relationship, your choices matter to your partner as well. The hours you work, where your job is located, the mood your work puts you in, your salary—even whether or not you need the family car to get to and from work—all affect your partner. While personal reflection is essential for all practical idealists, those in long-term relationships must examine their life choices with their partners. They are your most fundamental and essential community. Maintaining this tiny but powerful community requires making the choices that affect your practical idealism together. In the following pages, we look at three common dilemmas faced by practical idealists and their partners: where to live, finances, and how to cope with the demands of jobs that matter.

Where to Live

One of the hardest decisions for any couple to make, regardless of whether they are practical idealists, can be choosing where to live. One partner may have family ties in New York and the other in California or one may have a beloved job in Massachusetts while the other has a great career opportunity in Chicago. In our increasingly mobile society, these predicaments are commonplace, but for practical idealists it can be particularly difficult to reconcile the geographic needs of one partner with those of the other. For those working in nonprofits, for example, the reality is that a majority of large nonprofits are based in big coastal cities—particularly in New York and Washington, DC. On the other hand, local organizations and companies in smaller cities may offer one partner an ideal job, but the surrounding area may offer little by way of employment chances for the other partner. These are challenges that resist easy or painless solutions.

When asked, however, some of our partnered practical idealists were able to discuss their methods of addressing the problem of geography. While considering their next life phase and geographic location, Noah Merrill and his wife Natalie Baker Merrill, for example, agreed that they would move to wherever the other found a position—depending on who found a job first:

> While I was at the Peace Learning Center, I became involved with a woman who would become my partner and we were married just before we left the Midwest. We made the decision to move together. We realized there were opportunities that were opening up for us in Indianapolis, in social service agencies, things like that. We could either follow those opportunities as they presented themselves or we could really take a chance on the broader opportunities that were available. Both of us had a sense that we weren't being fulfilled, and wouldn't be fulfilled if we stayed. Both of us decided that we were going to put in a lot of job applications. We were going to look into a lot of different opportunities, graduate school, paid work, volunteer work, et cetera, both international and in the United States. Basically we were going to go wherever the first person landed a position. We didn't think it was going to be as ideal as this opportunity turned out to be. And when this [job with American Friends Service Committee Southeastern New England] happened things just started to fall into place. Natalie, my partner, went to graduate school in Vermont, and we moved to Rhode Island from Baltimore. I was living here [in Rhode Island] and she was living there [in Vermont] and it worked for us.

Noah and Natalie are now living together in Vermont. After leaving AFSC, Noah went to work with Iraqi refugees in Jordan. Natalie spent some time working in Jordan, as well; however, her primary position has been in Vermont where she works for the School for International Training. As of this writing, they are both living in the United States, though they are continuing their work with displaced Iraqis through the Direct Aid Initiative, which provides a mechanism for donated funds to pay directly for urgent medical care needed by specific refugees.

Reaching an agreement on where to live can have as much to do with temperament and outlook as choosing an appropriate location. When writer and statistician Paul Buckley decided to move from Chicago and a well-paying job to begin studying at Earlham School of Religion, a Quaker seminary, he made this choice jointly with his wife, Peg. It was a daring decision, but both of them shared a belief that things have a way of working out:

> I quit my job, Peg quit her job; we sold our house. We bought a new house in Richmond, Indiana [where the seminary is located]. We had no prospects for employment. When we went to downtown Richmond one time just on a lark, Peg stopped in the library. [Peg had once been a librarian.] Peg said, "You got any jobs open?" and they said "No we don't." Well, a week before we moved, when we actually got everything packed up and we were waiting for the truck to come, the phone rings and it was the library in Richmond saying "We have a job. Do you want to come work for us?" A week later we were signing the papers to buy our house and as soon as we were done with that she heads over to the library for an interview. We had a sense that God would provide when you're doing what you need to be doing.

The reality is that you can be a practical idealist anywhere, but only particular places will offer certain employment or educational opportunities. While both you and your partner might luck into ideal positions in the same town, it is perhaps more likely that there will need to be compromises when your generalized ambitions and hopes are mapped onto specific geographies. A conversation starter might be a version of this direct question: If you can't find a job that reflects your values where you live now, will your partner be willing and able to consider relocating? What if the reverse is true? As with all things practical idealist, serious reflection is required. The choices you two make matter not just to your practical idealism but to your long-term relationship.

Finances

If a practical idealist's passion leads her to a job that is meaningful and satisfying, but not particularly well compensated in financial terms, her choice directly affects her partner. In order to make ends meet, the couple might have to monitor their expenses carefully and, at times, do without. Alternatively, the other partner might have to assume the lion's share of responsibility for taking care of the family financially—perhaps working at a job that, while high paying, is not as satisfying as some jobs that might pay less. The key, once again, to avoiding resentment and misunderstandings is full and open discussion and disclosure.

Casey, a physician who is currently the sole breadwinner for her family while her husband, Nate, watches their two preschool children, says, "We talk about everything. It seems like our parents' generation does not talk about things as much or as openly as we do." Nate added, "It is important to set goals and establish priorities. This needs to be done together. Then it is easier to figure out what you can do to attain those goals. Once you have agreement on general goals, you can discuss the best path to be able to do what you want to do." The path couples chart will differ according to temperament and circumstances, but this doesn't matter as long as they both look at the map together and agree on their preferred route.

Tina and John, for example, followed a more traditional path—but both lived out their passion. John worked for nonprofits, while Tina taught elementary- and middle-school children. They mostly lived on John's salary, saving Tina's salary for extra or one-time expenses such as camp for their kids, vacations, and schooling. This meant keeping a close eye on expenses and a zealous commitment to savings. The checkbook was balanced each month, and family yearly budgets were mostly followed. Tina kept a sharp eye out for the family finances.

Ana, John's daughter, and her husband Jeff are following in John and Tina's footsteps. Jeff teaches and Ana works for a nonprofit. Ana says, "If you want to be a practical idealist, you have to limit your consumption and your spending. We don't go out much to eat and if we do we don't drink." Key to their success, she says, is making choices together as a couple, including their commitment to savings.

Questions for discussion:

1. What sort of financial agreements do you have, or plan to have, with your partner? How will the responsibility for paying living expenses be shared?

2. If one partner is the primary breadwinner, how does he or she feel about being in that position? Do they feel as if they're being denied an opportunity to pursue their own passions? How does the partner who is not the primary breadwinner feel?
3. If things seem unbalanced or inequitable now, is this a temporary or long-term situation?
4. Can you make a list of long-term financial goals and sketch out various routes to reach those goals?
5. What are your plans for following up on the answers to these questions? How often will you check back in and possibly adjust the answers, as they might alter as the goals and feelings of each person change? How well are you working towards the long-term goals you sketched out?

Emotional Costs of Your Job: Bringing Home the Angst Along with the Bacon

The importance of the community of support provided by your partner is perhaps nowhere more evident than when helping you cope with strains that may come with your practical idealist job. Particularly if both of you work at demanding jobs, you need, as practical idealist Dara Schulbaum told us, "safety and civility at home." While working as a therapist with kids who have emotional and behavioral problems, Dara had to contend with insurance bureaucracies and sometimes inadequate resources while doing her best to "soften the lives of these kids a little." She had to shoulder the burden of knowing that there are some children, like those born with fetal alcohol syndrome, who will never have it easy.

> I have seriously found myself in some of my worst moods getting off the phone with an insurance company because I can't believe them. The insurance company representative will be like, "I understand that he's hallucinating and...um...seeing warlocks on a daily basis and that he feels really depressed and he was suicidal, but you said he doesn't have a plan? Well, I'm not understanding why he needs to be in your program for five hours a day." And I'm like, "You've got to be kidding!" I've gotten off the phone so pissed off.

Dara and other practical idealists interviewed understand that having a practical idealist job that makes a difference and has positive consequences for social change can be a double-edged sword. Yes, such work is fulfilling, but it can also be draining. Annie Sartor knows that the nonprofit she works for, Oceana, is making a difference on the issue of ocean conservation. As the only organizer on the West Coast, she can see the results of her grassroots efforts to educate the public about the threat things like mercury poisoning and bottom trawling pose to the world's oceans. Annie told us, "I like going to work every day and knowing that I'm helping to preserve and protect the ocean." On the other hand, knowing that what you do means something makes it hard to shrug and say, "Never mind, it doesn't matter," when there are problems at work. If you are a lobbyist who is passionate about children's healthcare, for example, you are aware that even small details of federal healthcare legislation will determine whether or not a child has health insurance or not. This in turn can mean that an uninsured child suffers needlessly. The emotional and physical consequences of having such a demanding job will naturally affect your partner and your partnership.

At times, when one partner is feeling the effects of such stresses, the other partner acts as a sort of human "heat sink." A heat sink (a term from engineering) dissipates the heat from one part of a machine and allows that part to continue functioning. The chip in your laptop, for example, runs so hot and fast that it would melt were it not for the tiny heat sink and its fan. A "heat sink" partner may offer solutions or simply commiserate after a frustrating day on the job, but even heat sinks can become overwhelmed and overheated and burn out. When considering how your values are manifested in your work, it is also necessary to reflect, with your partner, if job stress is undermining the values that make you a good partner. If you are not the person you want to be after you leave work, what changes can you both make in order to ensure that you are able to live out your values both at your job and in your relationship?

Questions for discussion with your partner:

1. If you work long hours, when will you make time to spend with your partner?

2. Does your partner believe that you spend too much of your home time discussing or complaining about work? Does he or she mind being a "heat sink"?
3. How would you like your partner to support you when you have had a difficult day? Offer solutions? Not problem-solve but just commiserate?
4. How much of your work can you leave at the office?

Aretha's Favorite Word: R-E-S-P-E-C-T

Mutual respect is, of course, vital to all successful relationships, not just between practical idealists and their partners. Respect applies broadly to most aspects of any partnership, but practical idealists and their partners benefit from examining the issue of respect as it relates to their practical idealism and life choices. It is possible that one partner does not fully agree with or even understand the other's practical idealism, but, for the health of the relationship, it is vital that he or she respects it. Your partner cannot be a part of your community of support if he or she does not respect your commitment to practical idealism.

John once wrote about his thirty-plus years with Tina:

> Our marriage has worked because we have respected the need for each of us to live out our dreams—to be self-fulfilled by doing what we want to do. This has meant that we have each had to temper our visions to allow the other's room to grow. It has meant taking the time to be together, to enjoy each other's company, to talk and dream together. It has also meant not doing some things—such as taking certain jobs—that would strain the relationship past breaking. Marriage is a covenant, a commitment made. It tempers greed, individuality, egoism. It often leads where you would not have gone.

More questions:

1. Does your partner respect your commitment to practical idealism? Understand it? Share it? All of these are important but the one that is crucial is the first. People of different tem-

peraments, belief systems, or politics can be good partners, but only if they respect each other's choices.

2. Do you respect their point of view as well?

In order for practical idealist relationships to succeed, each member of this smallest of communities must remain open to the other. Decisions about where to live, finances, and how to cope with job stresses need to be made jointly, with each partner understanding the trade-offs involved. Particularly when both partners have their own careers, some choices are more difficult than if the decisions were being made by unconnected individuals. On the other hand, it is this very connection that makes it possible for many practical idealists to achieve what they could not on their own.

I Get By with a Little Help from My Friends: Your Friends and Your Practical Idealism

Practical idealists, like the rest of the population, can be extroverts, introverts, or somewhere in the middle. Some of the practical idealists we interviewed seemed to collect a large community of friends with little effort whereas others had smaller, but no less sustaining, groups of friends. Whether you revel in a hectic social calendar or prefer a more sedate homebody lifestyle, your friends are vital members of your community of support. In this section, we look at the various roles of friends in our interviewees' communities of support. We also consider how some of our practical idealists coped with having friends who did not support their practical idealism and the difficulty that busy practical idealists can have in maintaining friendships, as well as one approach to creating a community of friends when you move to a new town or city.

"The soul selects her own society," wrote Emily Dickinson, and practical idealists are no exception. Living as a practical idealist is not always easy and the practical idealists we interviewed reported a tendency to connect with others who were familiar with the various day-to-day challenges living as a practical idealist can present. Director of Environment North Carolina Elizabeth Ouzts told us, for example, that most of her friends chose "similar paths" and were able to "support each other during long hours for low pay." Other practical idealists confirmed the gravitational pull of mutual understanding. Josh Dorfman, who is both a practical idealist and an entrepreneur, recounted, "It can be lonely being an entrepreneur. People who aren't entrepreneurs don't have much of a sense of what it's like. So my two or three other friends who have started companies, we commiserate a lot. We understand each other."

Apart from providing emotional sustenance, friends can also give practical and relevant advice. The very experiences that allow them to sympathize with you also make them excellent sources of information. Dana Harrison, executive director of Dress for Success, told us that she gained a "degree by osmosis" while attending dinner parties with friends. Having never run a nonprofit before, Dana was able to "learn what worked and what didn't" around the supper table: "All of these endless hours of having dinner together and sharing a bottle of wine together and hearing them talk about their work and saying things like, 'Oh my gosh! Of course that fundraising didn't work because you didn't do this, this, this, and this.'" We will discuss this further in the next section on mentors, but for now it is worth underscoring that your friends are potentially the most diverse members of your community of support, and because of this, they offer you the chance to learn from experiences far different from your own.

Have you ever wondered why some women arrive at the Academy Awards in dresses that are so unflattering they make you wince? Our theory is that these poor souls must not have any real friends in Hollywood. They have no one to stop them at the dressing room door and say, "No way. You look like you're wearing a deflated beach ball. Take that off immediately." And just like a good friend with a good eye can give you fashion advice, a friend can be an alternative mirror who complements your own process of self-reflection. Good friends are truth tellers and they can sometimes see what you may have overlooked.

As an undergrad at UNC-Chapel Hill, Laura Hogshead planned to go to law school and work in legal aid until her friends came to her with another idea. "The Masters of Public Administration Program [at UNC] held an open house on campus, and they were sending out mass fliers. *Four* of my friends came up [to me] with this flier and said, 'This looks like you.'"

In physician Christiana Russ's case, it wasn't a specific program but a certain life path that friends mentioned to her. About the reflection of friends she says,

> It doesn't mean that they know the right answer for you, but they know a piece of you that might be useful. For instance, I had never considered the priesthood or doing anything in the church. I was an engineering student! I didn't even take any religion classes in college. Yet when I was working in that community, I started hearing from more and more different people there, "Oh, you should think about this." They saw me in that role, and it was not a role I ever thought of for myself. It was very eye-opening for me. I feel like I got to know myself better in a really good way. Friends see you even better than you see yourself.

It would be nice to imagine that all of your friends would respond positively to your practical idealism and the life choices that flow from it; however, in reality this is not always the case. Sometimes the disconnect is simply a consequence of having a job that does not fall within the traditional parameters of your peer group. In other words, your friends just don't "get" your job. Samantha Yu, who works for the City of Los Angeles, found that when she tried to explain her job in local government her friends would listen and then "they would say, 'Hmmm, ok.'" Her friends were curious, even asked questions, but they just didn't seem to fully understand her decision to work in government.

Jeff Deutsch describes another type of reaction that you might encounter from friends who are not practical idealists. "When I tell them what I do, even if I'm just first meeting someone, they seem to react in a way that almost assumes that I might disapprove of what they do, which is not the least bit true but I definitely get that from people." Similarly, as Josh Dorfman explains it, if you are met by silence when you tell someone what your plans are, you don't necessarily need to read disapproval into it: "When you tell someone that you're going to start this company or do this thing, you sometimes see something register on their face…what they're thinking is like, 'I could never do that,' or, 'Should I quit my job?' They just immediately go into their own head."

A key to parsing the responses of your doubting friends is listening to their objections (if they give voice to them) to hear if they may have a valid concern, but also to realize that sometimes what they are resisting is your implicit questioning of things as they are. As Josh Dorfman explains it, "When every step you are taking is challenging the status quo, you get messages like, 'Why don't you just go to law school?' or 'Why don't you just go get a job on Wall Street?' Then they'd be much more comfortable with you because they could relate to you." This does not mean that they might not be good friends in other respects or that you need to stop seeing them. Nonsupport of your practical idealist decisions is not the equivalent of undermining your choices. And if they do actively undermine or belittle something that is central to your core values and beliefs—then they probably are not particularly good friends anyway.

Not all of your friends will be involved in comparable work or adhere to practical idealist values. While many of our practical idealists reported that they tended to have friends who shared a broad interest in social change and whose jobs offered similar kinds of fulfillment and frustration, none of them claimed an exclusive community of idealist-only friends. Such a community would be a social monoculture and, in our opinion, isolating and unbalanced.

Nevertheless, while Jeff is right that practical idealists don't necessarily judge people in other professions harshly, issues can arise. It can be difficult to have friends who get paid superlative salaries when they are not working towards social change or if they are taking part in work that you deem harmful. This discomfort can be exacerbated if they suggest that they get paid more because their work is more demanding. They may not realize that practical idealist work can be just as arduous, and, more importantly, that much of the world works long and hard without even making a living wage.

Think of it as a "diversity issue." While you probably don't want to be friends with arms dealers, it's important to have a varied group of friends. Before jettisoning any friends, consider these questions: What do you get out of the friendship? Are you going to let go of a person who was a friend for ten years because they changed jobs?

Where do your values intersect? How important might it be to remain that person's friend and not lose the possibility of finding a moment to have at least one frank conversation about their work? Is it possible that you're losing out on different and valuable perspectives? Homogenous groups that lack dissenting views may be comfortable, but they don't reflect the broader community. And finally, as we pointed out earlier, remember that you are not a cause or a job and neither is your "wayward" friend.

The ways in which we can create friendships and community are almost infinite in their variety. In the words of E.M. Forster, "Only connect!" People can bond at book groups, the gym, Star Trek conventions, Revolutionary War re-enactments, and community bowling leagues. If you're a snob, you might deem some of these occasions lacking a certain gravitas, but those folks are out having a good time on weekends while you're surfing the internet and watching Cartoon Network. No person is any one thing; choose and keep friends that nurture different facets of your self.

It's necessary to keep blood and energy flowing to those different "parts" of your whole self in order to keep them alive. The friends Alissa met in dance class, for example, invited her to join a small dance company. This gave her a chance to choreograph, as well as be involved in outside work activities that were very important to her. On the other hand, having a varied friend group may also help you in finding new work. When Dress for Success director Dana Harrison decided to move back to Indianapolis, she had worked in both music and the private sector. Her Indianapolis friends, however, were generally in nonprofit organizations and one of them connected her to Dress for Success, which saw her potential.

At times, making friends is not the issue for practical idealists, instead, the trick lies in keeping those friendships current. Particularly if you are working long hours, it's easy to fall into a work-eat-sleep routine that isolates you from your friends and your community of support. A few of our practical idealists, for example, mentioned that they might get an email from a good friend and put it aside until they could "really answer" it with a nice, long response—and then, somehow, the email never got written. If this sounds at all familiar, remember that the time you put into sustaining your friendships is as vital as taking time to exercise, meditate, eat ice cream, or whatever self-care routine you practice. Your circle of friends work like smoke jumpers keeping you from becoming a burnt-out cinder of what once was a vibrant practical idealist.

While on the subject of burnouts, we want to flag one particular species of burnout that you may encounter in your community. They are what we call social change zombies—something inside them died and yet they keep on moving through the world. You may have spotted one in your travels—they hold hope and enthusiasm in disdain and intimidate others with their world-weary cynicism. And while these zombies don't eat brains, they do their best to suck the life out of practical idealists. You should be wary of them and their corrosive attitudes, but you do not need to be afraid of them. Your strong community network and robust habit of self-reflection will protect you from becoming one of them.

Question:

List your friends and how you met them. Have you stayed in touch with your old friends? Have you made new ones recently?

Making Friends after You Move

It may come as a surprise to learn that no one lives in New York City, Los Angeles, or Boston (or in Detroit, Raleigh, or Indianapolis, for that matter). In the end, everyone lives in a neighborhood or some community within a community. No place is as monolithic as it may first appear. Big cities can be as manageable as small towns, because each neighborhood has its own character and groups that form over causes or community events. These can also be great ways to meet people who are easy to socialize with because they live nearby. As a practical idealist, one of the ways to expand your circle or network is to get involved in helping to meet the community's needs. Finding the intersection of what the community needs and what interests you will help you meet people who share similar interests or abilities.

Karen, Alissa's mom, has long been involved in teaching African American history through the arts. In 2000 she moved from New York to Los Angeles to start a PhD program. Her first year in California, she joined the committee responsible for putting on a Juneteenth celebration in her city. (Juneteenth is the day of celebration for the emancipation of African American slaves.) While at an organizing committee meeting, she made a point that another woman agreed with and at the end of the meeting they ended up talking. Through the committee she met a number of women whom she now calls "sistah-friends." These friendships have supported her during her studies and some have led to paid work. (Networking through volunteering, as activist Annie Sartor and others pointed out, is especially common in the nonprofit sphere.) Karen did not become close friends with everyone around the table, but important bonds of her community were made through participation in that activity.

Help Me Obi-Wan: Mentors and Guides

When asked, all but one of our practical idealists could name at least one mentor who had provided essential guidance and advice. Often they could list several. While, like friends and family, mentors can be wellsprings of encouragement, mentors are also fonts of experience and skills. As your mentor, they make these skills and experiences available to you. They may act as sounding boards for your plans, write letters of recommendation, and help you navigate tricky situations on the job or in graduate school. At times the advice mentors provide may seem work-a-day or pedestrian, but this sort of guidance is often the most useful and practical. When netCorps outreach manager Aliya Abbasi moved from Chicago to North Carolina, a mentor not only took her around and showed her the sights, but also helped educate her in Southern decorum. Aliya came to understand that what was considered polite in the Windy City was not deemed so below the Mason-Dixon line. In order to make successful connections and contacts for her job, Aliya had to become fluent in an unfamiliar etiquette—and her mentor helped her to do this.

The mental image of a mentor that many of us carry around is that of a wisdom figure—something right out of Joseph Campbell or J.K. Rowling. If they're not Merlin or Albus Dumbledore, at least they are professors or well-established in their fields. But as Carmen Patrick Mohan and others of our practical idealists pointed out, mentors are not always your college professors or even someone much more experienced than you. Mackinnon Webster was leaving the country to work with the United Nations Development Program in Thailand when Alissa interviewed her. Mackinnon pointed out that a successful mentoring experience can often happen with someone just a little bit older or further down their career path than you. Such mentors may have recommendations and advice that will be both current and especially relevant to your situation. After all, they only recently embarked on this path themselves.

All this is not to say that professors or older colleagues are not to be sought out. Many of our practical idealists cited "traditional" mentor figures, as well. Attorney Torrey Dixon, for example, named his pastor, a torts professor, and a history professor. Law professor James Forman, Jr., recalls being profoundly influenced by lawyers at the NAACP and the Southern Center for Human Rights. Laura Hogshead said she had "dozens of mentors," people who "helped [her] see what was ahead of [her] and be less afraid of it." Although Laura had the good fortune to have an abundance of mentors, John notes that you don't actually need a lot of mentors—only a few trusted advisors with practical knowledge of your field.

When seeking out a mentor, however, be aware that the guidance that some mentors give may not be entirely unbiased or free from self-interest. Pediatrician Christiana Russ cautioned, for example, that what you want in a mentor is someone who has "your own interests at heart [and] who can see you in roles that perhaps you hadn't, and don't want to make you into a mini-me." A mentor, in other words, who genuinely "sees" you and is not simply leading you in a direction that validates his or her own life choices. Frankly, it is a rare thing to receive advice that has not been in some way influenced by the needs or hopes of the advice giver, and you will always need to "try on" the advice you receive to see if it truly makes sense for you. The best mentors will insist that you think for yourself and will offer support even when you strike out in a different direction than the one they have chosen. Attorney David Neal, for example, only learned *after* his Fair Trial Initiative had enjoyed some success that one of his mentors initially had believed that his nonprofit "was a harebrained scheme that we'd never be able to raise enough money for." Nevertheless, this professor, a true mentor, had refrained from belittling his initiative and supported his endeavor.

Question and activity:

Do you have a mentor/s? Create a list of names of possible mentors and how to contact them.

If you do not currently have a mentor in your field, take comfort in the fact that the people you will be approaching are often, in some fashion, practical idealists themselves. If it is a professor whom you are approaching keep in mind that a professor is a teacher. They want you to succeed. Some will be more responsive than others and almost all are very busy people. The fact that their calendars are full should not be a deterrent—it is most likely why they are enjoying the success they currently do. John, who has spent decades in the nonprofit and academic sectors, emphasizes that you cannot afford to allow shyness to get in the way of approaching a mentor. Take heart in knowing that even the most pompous twerp of a full professor or manager enjoys being asked for guidance. (Though, if you are certain that the professor is an arrogant git, then that person should not be a candidate for mentor, but, at best, a resource.) Remember as well Mackinnon's point about finding mentors who are closer to you in age.

If, like several of our interviewees, your interests are cross-disciplinary, you may find it a challenge to find a mentor who has knowledge relating to all the fields in which you hope to engage. Christiana Russ found it difficult, for example, as a physician interested both in international work and possible ordination in the Episcopal Church, to find appropriate mentors. "I can find people who are definitely very supportive, but it is hard to find people who have the same overlap that I do, which includes church work, international work, and medicine. I find that sometimes all of those different spheres don't really understand the other sphere." If you're like Christiana, then you may need more than one mentor in order to find the support you need.

Whomever you approach as a mentor, there are a few rules of mentor etiquette that will help you enjoy a successful relationship with that mentor.

1. Be respectful of your mentor's time. If you are dropping in during a professor's office hours or stopping by a mentor's

office for a chat, for example, do not overstay your welcome. Even if you are having a drink with a younger mentor, be sure to come prepared and keep your conversation from drifting too far or too long.

2. Be polite to the gatekeepers. If your mentor has an administrative assistant who schedules his or her appointments, be sure to be consistently and relentlessly courteous to him or her.
3. Say "thank you." Shoot your mentor an email after you've met. If your mentor has done something like introduced you to a job contact or taken you out for coffee, write a brief written note. This is not being sycophantic; it is showing that you appreciate the time and energy they have devoted to your benefit.

Finally, mentoring can also happen in the absence of a traditional mentoring relationship. Some of our practical idealists were mentored through workshops or books or by simply observing role models. Chris Estes, the executive director of the North Carolina Housing Coalition, for example, chose to attend Stone Circles just prior to entering graduate school. Stone Circles, Chris explained, had "faith, spirituality and social justice elements. It was all about helping younger people who were doing this social justice work to find spirituality and sustenance in that. That was a really important process for me too. It was a very intentional year, working with that group on a monthly basis. I was really thinking and reading books about where I should be and what's important."

Books also proved to be a guiding and sustaining force in the life of Dara Schulbaum, who eagerly told us of her latest book finds, *Soul of a Citizen* and *The Impossible Will Take A Little While*. "Those essays, oh my God, they're great. From those two books, he [Paul Rogat Loeb] seems like he really knows how to inspire people and keep them from burning out, which is such a pervasive problem. It's just amazing." "We read to know that we are not alone," a student tells C.S. Lewis in the play *Shadowlands*. Through reading, whatever the media, you can gain not only a mentor but also reassurance that you, too, are not alone.

Finally, if you are currently sans mentor, you can still create your own virtual mentor by paying close attention to the actions and choices of your chosen role models. Kelly Letzler, executive catering director of the Just 'Cause Catering arm of Second Helpings, told us, for example, "I haven't had one mentor. But I certainly have observed others in their careers and how they go about developing. A really strong influence is Jean Paison, one of the co-founders of Second Helpings. Her career is really neat. She started out in pastries, which is what I loved. She saw all the waste." (In response Paison started Second Helpings, a nonprofit that takes donated food and, using volunteer workers and a job-training program, prepares meals for about twenty different social service agencies in the area.) By following Ms. Paison and others, Kelly was mentored in her own practical idealist career.

Spiritual and Religious Groups

For some of our practical idealists, their faith or spiritual practices and the people these practices connect them to form fundamental communities of support. While participating in and receiving support from faith groups or spiritual practices is not essential to the idea of practical idealism, it was considered foundational by some our practical idealists. For Sanchia, Dara, Christiana, Noah, and others, these communities helped them set goals, reflect on their choices, and provided emotional, intellectual, and/or spiritual stamina and refreshment. Sanchia Patrick, for example, believes that "there is nothing more important to your well-being" than spirituality—that it is key for practical idealists to become "rooted"; likewise child therapist Dara Shulbaum told us that she felt anyone in her line of work would "benefit from some sort of spiritual practice." Christiana Russ's Episcopal discernment committee helped her determine not only whether she was being called to the ordained ministry but also helped her reflect on broader life issues.

Spiritual and religious groups can also provide more concrete forms of assistance. When she moved into a new town, Aliya contacted her local mosque to see if they had any information about housing in the area. Practical idealists and others have also found their congregations to be a source for job leads and personal recommendations.

The breadth and variety of spiritually focused communities are as diverse as practical idealists themselves. John, while objecting to and confronting the inflexible and discriminatory aspects of some parts of the institutional church, still attends.

> I find the community of faith to be important. I worship in a small, diverse, bilingual urban church, where I interact constantly with people from different classes, races, ethnicities, and cultures. We certainly do not all have the same interpretation of our Christian faith, but over time we have built a sense of community, a sense of belonging, and a sense of care and understanding among us. It is important for me to be able to share with a community broader than just my immediate family. The church offers me that opportunity. It offers me a place where I feel safe to laugh and to cry, to sing and to speak out. I know that I will be accepted. The church is a community of faith that supports me and is with me in my daily life.

Spiritual practices like yoga and Zen meditation, which can be done in a group or in solitude, have also been important to some of the practical idealists we interviewed. Religion and spirituality are, obviously, a matter of personal choice and of finding what does or does not resonate as true in your own life. Whether or not it proves true for you, spiritual communities have given vital support to many practical idealists.

Question:

If there is a spiritual practice with which you feel comfortable and that connects you to a larger community of support, have you taken the steps necessary to ensure that you can remain engaged and involved with that community?

COLLEAGUES AND PROFESSIONAL NETWORKS

Your work colleagues and the professional networks to which you belong are another critical part of your community support. Sanchia Patrick found a job through the Atlanta Marketing Association, where she served on the Young Professionals Committee. Sarah Haller learned about her future employer, the Greening of Detroit, while attending a conference for the National Association for Interpretation, an organization for interpreters of natural and cultural resources. Amanda Edmonds of the community garden nonprofit,

Growing Hope, received valuable support from the Detroit Agricultural Network. While occupational networks primarily foster only work-related connections and professional development, colleagues can be mentors or friends in addition to being work associates. Regardless of their role, you will almost inevitably be spending a lot of your waking hours in the company of your coworkers, so whether or not your workplace offers a genuine community of support is a key to the success of your work as a practical idealist. Walker Coppedge, director of graduate support at Epiphany School in Dorchester, Massachusetts, for example, reports that the teachers and colleagues he has met at the school have become good friends with whom he socializes outside of work. Walker appreciates having a community of friends who are "like-minded" and believes that his practical idealist job has provided him with a community of friends that he would not have found at another job. By contrast, Dana Harrison left her position as a music teacher at an elementary school in part because as the school's only music teacher she found herself isolated: "I found myself wishing that I had other colleagues there that I could just talk to about what we were doing and building—on the day in day out basis."

It seems obvious, but it bears emphasizing—your colleagues and workplace setting have an enormous impact on the successful implementation of your personal goals as a practical idealist. Jeff Deutsch, a graphic designer at Oxfam, was motivated and inspired by his work alongside colleagues who were well-informed and broadly experienced:

> I was hearing about increased conflict in the Democratic Republic of the Congo on the news.... I walked into the office of one of the writers I work with a lot and I said, "Hey Chris, have you been following this? I don't really know very much about the DRC, do you know anything about it?" And he turns to me and says, "Well, in the sixties, the Belgians pulled out of the DRC..." I had a 15-, 20-minute crash course history lesson on the DRC since the 1960s. Where am I going to learn that other than at a place like this? What kind of working environment can you go in and learn about these things? Or work with people who are coming back from Sri Lanka after the tsunami or are trying to resolve border conflicts in northern Ethiopia

> and Eritrea. When I wake up in the morning and occasionally I hear one of my friends on NPR talking about the work that we're doing, it's incredibly uplifting. It's really inspiring and it's definitely a motivator.

Question:

How would you evaluate your current community of support at work? If there are deficits, could you team up with someone to start something that would increase community?

South African anti-apartheid playwright Athol Fugard once said that the central arena of history is the relationship between one man or woman to another man or woman. Practical idealists may have big ideals and large causes, but social change comes down to societies of individuals. Community is fundamental. Practical idealists know that personal change and social change are interconnected and that this connection works both ways. Practical idealists work to sustain and improve society, but at the same time their own society nourishes and strengthens them. After struggling to balance the demands of his practical idealist mission with his own needs and the needs of his community, Noah Merrill concluded: "People who believe that they are saving the world by sacrificing their children or their relationships or themselves are ultimately going to do damage to themselves and everyone else."

6. Choosing Matters

There are many more stories of practical idealists and their choices than could ever be included in one book. All over the country—all over the world, really—practical idealists are doing amazing work for social change. It's time for you to join them. In the preceding chapters, we have discussed many of the choices that *you* must consider in order to live as a practical idealist. There are decisions to be made about the specific type of work you want to pursue, how to manage your debt and meet your financial obligations, how to repurpose your existing talents, and what kinds of new skills you need to develop. There are also questions about how to create and maintain a consistent reflective process and remain connected to the community that supports you.

Some of these choices may result in big decisions: a move across the country, enrollment in graduate school, or starting your own business. Other choices—perhaps taking a colleague out to lunch to glean career ideas or deciding to pay an extra $40 each month on your student loan—are less earthshaking. Whether the decision is large or small, however, practical idealism requires that you act—with alacrity. Choices matter, yes, but *choosing* matters even more.

We know choosing isn't easy. Even after engaging in your own careful reflection and analysis, choices can rarely be made with absolute certainty. You won't always have all of the information you think you need to make a decision. You might worry that there are too many variables and that something is likely to go horribly awry. Just remember that "perfection is the enemy of the good." People, particularly very smart people, can always figure out a reason to avoid taking action, and the smarter they are, the more articulate their rationalizations for inertia will be. There will always be something to distract you from making your choices. Choose anyway.

When doubts and anxiety creep into your thoughts, we hope that you will find encouragement and comfort in the stories of the practical idealists in this book. Their narratives demonstrate that you can follow your passion, live a life focused on more than maximizing your income, work for positive social change, and survive financially. They too have had debts to pay and partners to consult. They have felt under-qualified and under-networked, had hard conversations about money, and fretted about where to live. They've asked themselves whether it's all worth it and whether they're making a real difference. They have survived all of this and thrived. You can, too. You can live, and live well, as a practical idealist. Choose now to make your choices matter.

A Note on Higher Education

Attending college or graduate school is not a prerequisite for being a practical idealist, but education experiences *were* essential for many of the practical idealists we interviewed. When you're a student, invaluable practical idealist experiences are found both inside and outside the classroom. While at Oberlin College, Rachel Weidenfeld took a paid internship teaching English as a second language to Mexican farm workers. She got lost many times driving to class sites in the Ohio countryside, but eventually learned to navigate the back roads and earned the respect of thirty-five skeptical students. Her experiences working in diverse communities served her well in her job with a social service organization in Massachusetts. Aliya Abbasi's work-study job at her college's computer lab led her to a position with netCorps after she graduated. In-classroom experiences inspired David Neal to found a nonprofit devoted to the civil rights of criminal defendants while still in law school.

As the examples above show, college for the practical idealist is about much more than coursework. As a practical idealist, you must pursue your education, both in and out of the classroom, with deliberate purpose. It is not enough to think that a degree might be helpful to your career in some general way. Before you apply, you need to determine not only which degree will help you in your work, but also how programs and opportunities available to you while in school will advance your career and practical idealism.

Questions for those considering college:

1. How does your chosen field of study relate specifically and concretely to your future as a practical idealist?
2. While in school, what activities, in addition to coursework, do you plan to pursue to further your career goals? Do the schools you're considering have an abundance of student organizations, internships, or work co-op programs relevant to your practical idealism? Look at an events calendar for your potential school. Does your campus attract speakers or host events that will broaden and deepen your educational experience?
3. Your school's financial aid department should be able to tell you the average amount of debt owed by students upon graduation. Particularly if you are considering an advanced degree, are you reasonably certain that your salary after graduation will allow you to make your loan payments on time?

SPECIAL ISSUES FOR THOSE CONSIDERING GRADUATE OR PROFESSIONAL SCHOOLS

After college, many practical idealists return to academia, at some point, to pursue advanced degrees or professional training. If you too are considering a post-bachelors education, remember that it is not enough to imagine that a graduate education might be helpful to your career in some general way. Before you apply, you need to determine not only which degree will help in your work, but also how programs and opportunities available to you while in school will advance your career and practical idealism.

Sue Erhardt, education director for Greening Detroit, was clear, for example, that she did not want to go to grad school just to do research that would further the careers of her professors but not necessarily her own career. With this last concern in mind, she took care to have her thesis and choice of advisor accepted before she began coursework at the University of Michigan–Dearborn. As Sue puts it, "I basically wanted my advisor to help me in my own research instead of the other way around."

Question:

If you already have a bachelors or associates degree, what specific opportunities do you see an additional degree opening up? Research people who already inhabit the sort of career you envision yourself having. What degrees do they have on their resume?

AFTER YOU'VE MADE THE DECISION TO GO

The practical idealists we interviewed understood how to use the systems of which they were a part, including educational systems. In this case, there is nothing nefarious about exploiting resources. Our practical idealists figured out what educational assets and possibilities existed at their universities and used them to their own benefit. In order that you might be able to do likewise, in this brief note we have organized the diverse educational experiences of our practical idealists into seven broad categories. The categories are:

- Research
- Courses
- Training and internships
- Study abroad and overseas experiences
- Institutional resources
- Leaves of absence
- Direct social change work

Research

Practical idealists often find creative ways to connect college and graduate school research assignments with their particular interests and passions. John, for example, wanted to study Latin America while in grad school, but, in the late 1960s at the Fletcher School, there weren't many courses offered specifically on that region of the world. John solved this by completing all of the research assignments from his law, politics, and economics courses by doing research papers that concentrated on development issues in Latin America.

Research can also help you uncover what your interests are. As an undergraduate, attorney Torrey Dixon attended Averett University in his hometown of Danville, Virginia. While in school, he began doing research on the history of civil rights in Danville and learned that Danville had been "one of the central areas in the civil rights movement." Torrey told Alissa, "That moved me into studying about the civil rights movement, which drew me more into the civil rights area of law. That's what I think led to my transition from being a student of history to wanting to be an actual role player in a political scene. And that's when I decided to go to law school."

Courses

It should be obvious, but it bears repeating: the chief glory and privilege of college is the chance to learn and to explore. Often, just one class can change your life. It is a colossal mistake not to let your intellectual curiosity range far and wide during your undergraduate career. Many of our practical idealists have similar stories to Mel Rodis, whose career path was heavily influenced by a course she took in international human rights. "I thought: 'This is what I want to do with my life.' I decided I wanted to be a human rights lawyer." Sanchia Patrick, by contrast, described not a class, but a guest lecturer. "A woman came to speak to my journalism class. She was really sharp. She talked about how to develop your portfolio as a college student and how to present your portfolio to companies that are looking to hire." Sanchia took those tips and applied for an internship with that very woman. She got the internship and that led to her first job when she graduated from college.

For attorney David Neal, mentioned above, it was not one lecture or one class that had the major impact. Instead, it was a diverse curriculum that allowed him to take courses in immigration and refugee asylum law, as well as classes geared towards future public defenders. He was also taught by professors with an abiding interest in social justice, like Richard Rosen of The Innocence Project and Jack Boger, who had been head of the NAACP's Capital Punishment Project. It was here that David gained a much deeper understanding of the death penalty and its inequities. He says, "I just felt like that was where I could do the most good and where there was the most dire need for more resources." As you know, David went on to found the Fair Trial

Initiative, which is "dedicated to making sure that people who are facing the death penalty get outstanding representation."

Practical idealists may also be able to design their own curriculum. Quaker organizer and nonprofit founder Noah Merrill, for example, created his own major in cross-cultural conflict transformation. He knew that standard political science, economics, and sociology were not for him or, as he put it, "Certainly an all-Western approach is one that has not really fit with me very well." Though it took additional effort and paperwork, Noah believes his major helped him "cultivate new ways of looking at things."

Training and Internships

Most colleges and graduate schools offer a variety of special training sessions, weekend retreats, and career counseling workshops, in addition to traditional classes. These resources are often already covered by your tuition. Make it your mission to ferret out what extracurricular activities are available and use those that you think will be helpful. At Northwestern University, for example, Sarah Bush, co-executive director of Americans for Informed Democracy, participated in the Freshman Urban Program as part of her freshman orientation. "I hit the ground running and just realized how important I thought being engaged in service activities was. It shaped my college experience." It also laid the foundation for her continued passion for service after college.

At Tufts University, John has been heavily involved with Tisch College's Citizenship and Public Service Scholars Program, which works with undergraduates to help them develop leadership skills. Citizenship and Public Service Scholars act as catalysts in the general student population, engaging peers and faculty in the values and activities of active citizenship. Through individual and group projects, scholars contribute to improving conditions in communities at Tufts and in the larger world. Amherst College, Alissa's alma mater, is setting up a similar citizenship program for its students.

Retreats and workshops have also become increasingly popular across many college campuses. Denison University, for example, sponsors the Quest Program for its sophomores. This weekend retreat is designed to help second-year students think about their future lives and about how they can best use their time at Denison in the service of that future. Other educational institutions offer spiritual or meditative retreat opportunities. Georgetown University, for example, sponsors retreats geared specifically towards its Catholic, Protestant, Muslim, Jewish, Orthodox Christian, and secular students through its Campus Ministry Department.

In addition to training opportunities and retreats, internships were frequently cited by our practical idealists as key influences on their career choices. Many internships are either unsalaried or pay only a small stipend, so students may need to get an additional paying job to make ends meet.

Internships can change your whole orientation and point your life in an entirely new direction. Samantha Yu majored in political science at Berkeley. Interested in political theory, she always thought she would "seek a masters or potentially a doctorate in political science." Instead, however, she took an internship in the mayor's office of the City of Los Angeles: "It made me think, 'Well, do I really want to go into theory or do I want to go into something more hands-on?'" This experience was instrumental in Samantha's decision to enter the Masters of Public Policy program.

Another of Samantha's internships was equally valuable because it helped her clarify what she did not want to do. While Samantha was earning her masters degree, she interned for a school board member in the Los Angeles Unified School District (LAUSD). While it was "stressful" trying to juggle her academic and internship commitments, Samantha benefited from learning that she was not cut out to work in the district, especially for an elected board member. "As much as I enjoyed the work and I appreciated the partnerships and the relationships that I had, I decided at that point 'This is not for me.'"

As an undergraduate, Laural Horton accepted a political science internship with an attorney who worked with female prisoners who had been assaulted by their prison guards. Her supervisor acted as a mentor and gave her both responsibility and latitude in her work assignments. This internship was one of the primary reasons Laural chose to go to law school after college.

Study Abroad and Overseas Experiences

Like internships, study abroad programs also proved essential to many of our practical idealists. It's pretty much a cliché how much study abroad can challenge your worldview and reshape your values and philosophy of life. Cliché or not, however, living overseas does have an enormous effect on those who do so—particularly when the places visited differ sharply from home. Sarah Bush, for example, studied in England during her junior year abroad, but the most transformative part of her experience was not Oxford, but her travels in Europe and Northern Africa. "It was an eye-opening experience. I made a lot of friends who were not American." In Moroccan souks, she saw Nike-clad youths listening to familiar rap music next to Moroccans in traditional dress. The differences between explicitly tourist sites and other parts of Marrakech were stark. It was also evident that Moroccan women enjoyed far less freedom of movement than their male counterparts. Sarah had had internships in the United States, but this experience overseas made her realize that she wanted to work on international issues.

The international experiences of our practical idealists did not always come as part of a study abroad program. A number of those we interviewed had life-changing experiences overseas, but they were not organized around a study abroad program. Noah Merrill took a bus from Chicago to the southern end of Mexico and back again. He had combined the money he had saved while working as a manager of a local food co-op with a small grant from his university and hopped a bus to Chiapas. The long bus trip, he said, "was part of the journey. I wanted to pass through the different cultural zones and experience a small part of what people who migrate up through Mexico experience."

Eric Greitens was a teacher in China and worked in refugee camps in Croatia and Rwanda. Eric, too, had received a small travel grant while in college. He went first to China where he taught English. He was nineteen, had never been overseas before, and was arrested for teaching about human rights in one of his classes. "It really brought home to me the reality of political rights and civil rights and what they really meant in the United States." The next summer he lived and worked in refugee camps where he gained a "a real firsthand appreciation for the challenges that face people who want to do humanitarian work abroad." His third summer, he traveled to Rwanda where he helped provide services to unaccompanied minors. Eric sums up the impact of all these international experiences that shaped his practical idealism this way: "It was a combination of all of those experiences and the examples of Professor Boothby, Jason, Caroline, and some of the other volunteers whom I had met that really helped me know I wanted to focus my study on those kinds of humanitarian issues."

Physician Christiana Russ found that a self-planned trip to Guatemala helped her confirm where her passions lay.

> My fourth year of med school I went to Guatemala for a month—just because I really wanted to go to a developing country to see what medicine was like there. I went with this Mayan midwife to the highlands and had the most incredible experiences with her. I really loved it. I already had an interest in health policy and research, but had only done a little bit of that domestically. After that experience in Guatemala, I really became interested in international medicine.

Using University Resources

Most practical idealists discover to some degree how to use the resources available at their colleges and universities. We have already seen examples of finding college monies to finance travel or civic experiences. In another example of creative use of university resources, Amanda Edmonds worked out how to use student government funds and some fellowship money to launch her community garden program. Amanda also was able to mobilize undergraduate students both as interns and as community-based research fellows. After graduation, she worked at the University of Michigan and was able to sign off on these students getting credit for this work. In addition, because she had worked as an academic advisor and recruiter for the School of Natural Resources, she was able to earn her masters while setting up her nonprofit: "Someone offered me a teaching position for a semester, which waived my tuition and gave me money and full health insurance...I figured I could get a graduate degree while I was at it."

Sasha Chanoff entered the Fletcher School of Law and Diplomacy knowing he wanted to start a nonprofit. He felt he needed a graduate degree to give him credibility, but he wanted his own organization to work on refugee resettlement issues in Africa. Sasha made sure he took John's course on NGO management. The semester-long assignment was to build a nonprofit—from mission statement to budget, from personnel policies to operational plans. Sasha went to work with his passion, and by the end of the semester, he had a planning document that allowed him to begin raising funds for his nonprofit, Mapendo.

Xanthe Scharff and Rinn Self were also students at the Fletcher School. While working as a project evaluator for CARE in Malawi, Xanthe had seen the lack of educational opportunities for young girls. In response, she organized fellow students as volunteers, got an article in a newspaper that helped her raise some funds, and started a nonprofit, AGE (the Advancement of Girls Education Scholarship Fund). Xanthe and Rinn deftly mobilized the labor, resources, and accounting systems of the university to support her fledgling organization. Xanthe convinced her professor and advisor to adopt the program for a year while she secured nonprofit status and maintained the program with student volunteers. Today AGE offers secondary school scholarships, mentoring, and leadership training for girls in rural Malawi so they can continue their education.

Taking Time Off

A few of the practical idealists we met felt that it was important not just to take time to reflect on what was meaningful, but also that it was necessary to take some time off from academia to give yourself an opportunity to catch up with your thoughts and emotions. Christiana Russ, for example, knew when she left the University of Washington that she needed some time off. She, however, was just not sure how to go about this sabbatical from school, so she approached her priest with her tentative plans: "He sent out this wonderful blanket letter to people that he knew. Through this, I found out about the Micah Project, which is a discernment program within the church. It was through this program that I came to Boston for a year, deferring medical school." Christiana worked half-time doing social change work and came out of the year knowing that she really wanted to combine her medical degree with her passion for social justice.

In college, Alissa's friend, Sonali, took a semester off, much to the chagrin of her family. Sonali was interested in international development and wanted to have a clearer vision of how she could fit into the development world after college. During her leave of absence, Sonali spent time in India working for the Self Employed Women's Association. After college, she built on this work after winning a Thomas J. Watson fellowship, which provides travel grants for independent study outside of the United States. After two years working as a consultant in the private sector, Sonali found herself helping the Clinton Foundation open their office in India.

Social Change Work

Service opportunities and social activism, whether at home or abroad, are abundantly available for college students. There are structured programs that may last for a week or a year, as well as less formal arrangements. Annie Sartor went to the University of Seattle in part because she knew the WTO protests were scheduled to take place there, but her activism did not end with those marches. She became very involved in the anti-globalization movement, and she volunteered for Greenpeace doing climate change work. Annie also focused on sweatshops and anti-war organizing. This activism led directly to her work after college as an organizer; her skill set was unique because of all the experience she had accumulated at the university.

While studying political science at Antioch College in Ohio, Marie Trigona participated in a co-op program where she worked with refugees inside an INS detention center in Florence, Arizona. She later started another co-op, this time in Argentina. This co-op didn't work out, but she ended up doing a documentary project and learning about independent media. After graduation, Marie returned to Argentina where she made connections with an activist group that promoted workers' rights and began work as a writer and videographer.

Sonia Ramian's activism was quite different. As a student at the Fletcher School at Tufts University, she launched a one-person campaign to get her school to use fairly traded coffee in its cafeteria. Sonia enlisted professors, talked to the dining service, and spoke with the dean. She persisted even when she was told that it was too expensive and that the unionized cafeteria workers would not be able to do the extra work. She talked all the way to the president of the university and met every objection that was raised. She demonstrated that all of the arguments used to block the project were either untrue or could be overcome. At last she was successful, and her school now serves fairly traded coffee.

Being Efficient about Your Education

Idealism has traditionally flourished inside academic institutions, but practicality, particularly for practical idealists, must play an equal role. While getting the best education possible, price and speed are two elements to take into consideration. Attorney Alycia Guichard, for example, started her undergraduate education at Westchester Community College. She changed her major from sociology to communications in order to qualify for a scholarship offered by New York University's School of Education. Alycia, who knew she wanted to attend law school, calculated that her change of majors would allow her to follow her passions while taking on much less debt. In the speed department, after studying restaurant management at Purdue, Kelly Letzler of Just 'Cause Catering knew she wanted to attend culinary school. "I did some research on culinary schools. Having just spent four years at a university, I asked, 'What's the quickest avenue to get this degree, to get this completed?' I found a culinary school in Portland, Oregon—the Western Culinary Institute.…Eight hours a day, six days a week, that was our class, but it was done in a year."

The reason we're talking about speed and efficiency isn't because we don't appreciate all the glorious benefits of being in school. Although we talk about this in much more detail in our finances chapter, we just wanted to remind you to be clear about why and how you are incurring education debt. If your loan burden is too high after you graduate, then certain practical idealist jobs, especially those at entry level, might prove impossible to accept because they won't pay enough to cover your monthly student loan payments. If school is taking you longer because you're participating in internships or co-ops, getting international experience, or doing innovative but time-consuming research, more power to you! Just make sure that this educational path jibes with your future goals.

Conclusion

As a practical idealist, you must approach your education strategically. If you are considering college or graduate school or are already in school, now is the time to act in order to take full advantage of opportunities offered while pursuing your degree.

With deepest apologies to Henry David Thoreau, a practical idealist's motto in college might sound something like this: "I went to college because I wanted to learn deliberately. I wanted to live deep and suck out all the marrow of learning...to put to rout all that was not learning; and not, when I came to graduate, discover that I had not learned." While in college or graduate school, give yourself every chance to have those "Aha!" moments. You are preparing yourself for work and life, yes, but be certain you're taking every opportunity to discover exactly what kind of life you as a practical idealist genuinely want.

Appendix 1: Practical Idealism Project Biographies

Aliya Abbasi works to bridge the digital divide as the Basebuilding Initiative Project Coordinator at netCorps. At the time of her interview, Aliya was serving at netCorps in the capacity of Technology Outreach Manager in Greensboro, NC. In this AmeriCorps VISTA position she was able to combine her educational background in computers and interest in technology with her desire to volunteer.

Allison Greenwood Bajracharya is currently the Managing Director of District Strategy for Teach For America, Los Angeles. Previously, after completing her commitment with Teach For America in New Orleans as a corps member and receiving a Masters in Public Policy, Allison worked as the Director of Community Affairs for the Los Angeles Unified School District's Board President, Marlene Canter.

Kenan Bigby is a Project Manager at Trinity Financial where he oversees the development of building projects to revitalize neighborhoods. Before joining Trinity, Kenan worked on issues of affordable housing development and management. Kenan has a Bachelors in Sociology with a focus on urban planning.

Paul Buckley is a Quaker historian and theologian who spends most of his time "writing big books for a small audience and losing money." Before attending the Earlham School of Religion, a Quaker seminary in Richmond, Indiana, Paul worked full-time on national surveys and studies in health and education. Twelve years later, he and his wife "survive by the grace of God."

Sarah Bush is currently a PhD candidate in international relations in the Department of Politics at Princeton University. She was Co-Executive Director of Americans for Informed Democracy (AID) at the time of her interview. Sarah has also worked for the US State Department, St. Louis City Mayor's Office, and Teach For America.

Sasha Chanoff is founder and Executive Director of the humanitarian organization Mapendo International. Before launching Mapendo, he consulted with the Office of the UNHCR in Kenya and worked with the International Organization for Migration throughout Africa, identifying refugees in danger, undertaking rescue missions, and working on refugee protection issues.

Walker Coppedge became Associate Director of Admissions for Access and Retention at Tufts University in 2007. In this capacity, he helps use Tufts as a resource to promote college access in and around Boston. Previously, Walker was the Director of Graduate Support and Athletic Director at Epiphany Middle School, where he helped students from low-income Boston families transition to and succeed in high school.

Kristen DeRemer is currently an independent consultant on issues related to gender, conflict, and human security. Prior to this, she worked with women and girls affected by conflict in Northern Uganda and as a Research Consultant for professors at the Fletcher School and for the Feinstein International Center. Other experiences include work in Rwanda, Uzbekistan, and some "hollow-feeling stuff" for a corporation in New York.

James de la Vega is a graffiti artist, painter, photographer, educator, activist, and thinker from Spanish Harlem. He is well known for creating art in public spaces, including murals and chalk drawings on the streets of New York City. At the beginning of his career, James taught for a few years in a New York City grade school.

Jeff Deutsch is the Design Manager at the international relief and development organization Oxfam America. He manages a team of designers and freelancers and designs print and online materials that promote Oxfam's anti-poverty and social justice work. Jeff has been working as a graphic designer in print and interactive media since earning a Bachelors in Philosophy from Connecticut College.

Torrey Donell Dixon is currently the Director of FairVote North Carolina. At the time of his interview, he was a fellow at the University of North Carolina Center for Civil Rights, working mostly on voting rights and services for communities excluded from annexation in North Carolina. Torrey has also worked as a legal research assistant with the Southern Christian Leadership Conference and served as a clerk with the Danville Circuit Court in Virginia.

Josh Dorfman works to make environmentalism relevant to a wide array of people. He uses his MBA as founder and CEO of Vivavi, which works with leading environmental designers to provide contemporary, eco-friendly furniture and furnishings. In 2006, Josh launched ModernGreenLiving.com, which helps consumers find green homes and green building experts in North America. Josh is also the author of *The Lazy Environmentalist: Your Guide to Easy, Stylish, Green Living.*

Amanda Maria Edmonds is founder and Executive Director of Growing Hope. Growing Hope helps individuals, groups, and communities build capacity through community and school gardening programs that focus on growing, health and nutrition, and environmental sustainability. Growing Hope also runs an urban farmers' market as part of its work around healthy food access.

Sue Erhardt became Education Director of Casey Trees in September 2007. Previously, she served as Education Director and Governmental Liaison for the Greening of Detroit for nine years. In Detroit, she created an environmental education program that was instituted throughout the Detroit Public Schools. The goal of the program is to increase environmental science skills among children through outdoor exploration, creating the next generation of environmental stewards.

Chris Estes is the Executive Director of the North Carolina Housing Coalition, a nonprofit advocacy and resource organization focused on housing and community development issues for low- and moderate-income North Carolinians. His varied career includes work on housing development, fundraising for youth and early childhood development issues, and rural economic development.

James Forman, Jr., is a Professor at the Georgetown University Law Center where he teaches and writes about criminal procedure and education law. He is also the co-founder and Board Chair of the Maya Angelou Public Charter School in Washington, DC, which holds high standards for students in lower income urban areas.

Peter Girard is a Senior Analyst on the Environmental Stewardship Team at the Timberland Company. He assesses the environmental footprint of the company's business units and helps to focus its resources on environmental programs. Peter holds a Masters of Science in Resource Administration and Management and a Bachelors in Chemistry with a concentration in environmental science.

Yolanda González is a history teacher at the Moses Brown School in Providence, RI. Yolanda began her teaching career after working as a social worker in Philadelphia's inner-city schools and seeing that the bar for education needed to be higher. She challenges her students to become aware of the world around them and to work towards finding their place in the world so that they become active members in our society.

Eric Greitens served as a White House Fellow from 2005 to 2006. As a fellow, Eric founded the Universities Rebuilding America Partnership to enable colleges and universities to assist communities affected by the 2005 Atlantic hurricanes. After his fellowship year, Eric served in Iraq as the Commander of an Al Qaeda Targeting Cell. When he returned home, Eric founded the Center for Citizen Leadership, a nonprofit organization that gives fellowships to wounded and disabled veterans to begin new careers in public service.

Alycia Guichard is the Interim Director of the Minority Student Program and Externships and Supervising Attorney and New Jersey Bar Fellow for the Street Law Program at the Rutgers University School of Law. At the time of her interview, she was the Graduate and Clinical Teaching Fellow for the Street Law Clinic at the Georgetown University Law Center.

Sarah Haller is the Director of Environmental Education at the Greening of Detroit. She uses her environmental studies degree to direct education programs that help Detroiters replant their communities and learn about nature. Originally from California, Sarah served as an AmeriCorps member in Los Angeles.

Casey and **Nate Hanson** are married and live in Maine. Nate left a PhD program at MIT to train as a furniture maker and is currently a stay-at-home Dad taking care of their two children. Casey is a family physician working ¾ time at Maine Coast Memorial Hospital.

Tambra Harris is a choreographer, musician, and lead drummer with GIWAYEN MATA, an award-winning, soul-stirring, all-sistah, dance, percussion, and vocal ensemble. Tambra also uses her degree in exercise science to bring healthy living to African American communities by teaching dance throughout Atlanta.

Dana Harrison is the Executive Director of Dress for Success Indianapolis. The injustices of poverty and the needs of women in her community have become her passion during her time with the organization. She had previously worked in the fields of human resources, financial management, and music education. Outside of work she remains active in early and sacred music.

Robert Helfenbein works on issues related to urban education and cultural studies as a teacher of teachers. He is Assistant Professor of Teacher Education at Indiana University–Indianapolis and Associate Director of the Center for Urban and Multicultural Education (CUME). Before becoming a professor, Robert was a middle school and high school social studies teacher.

L. Scott Hilliard is Executive Director of Try-Again Homes in Washington, Pennsylvania. Try-Again Homes is "a private, nonprofit corporation committed to providing safe nurturing places for children in need and dedicated to the growth, development, and empowerment of individuals and families for healthier communities."

Nicole Hoagland has unleashed her passion for social justice by advocating for adolescent girls in state custody, battered women and their children, and LGBTQ youth over the last ten years. At the time of her interview Nicole was the Youth Program Director at Time Out Youth. She celebrates the incredible strength of character and tremendous willingness of people to take risks in order to successfully create a partnership that works.

Laura Hogshead was the Assistant Director of the Center on Poverty, Work and Opportunity at the University of North Carolina, Chapel Hill. She, along with the Director, Senator John Edwards, helped steer the organization whose goal is to bridge the gap between academics and activists working on poverty issues. She is currently on the professional staff of the United States House of Representatives Appropriations Subcommittee on Transportation, Housing and Urban Development.

Laural Horton was an asylum attorney at Freedom House in Detroit, Michigan, at the time of her interview. She provided legal services as part of the organization's comprehensive services for people seeking asylum in the United States and refugee status in Canada. Laural is an avid traveler.

Ana Hammock Isen is an adult educator in the field of financial literacy at ACCION USA. She teaches seminars on credit and money management to immigrants throughout New England. She has worked as a paralegal and fundraiser for a Latino community organization in Boston. She also spent a year working in Sri Lanka after the tsunami with tea plantation laborers on human rights issues.

Jeff Isen is a high school teacher at Boston Latin Academy. He worked on relief and development programs in Malawi, Sri Lanka, Uganda,

Mozambique, and Egypt before becoming a high school teacher. He has a Masters in International Relations and a Bachelors in Environmental Studies and English.

Brandie A. Ishcomer is a Management Assistant for the City of Phoenix Library Department. She works with library staff and the Library Advisory Board to support libraries in their promotion of community development through literacy. Brandie also works on constituent issues with the City Manager's Office and the City Council and Mayor's offices.

Jennifer Jordan is on a journey to find her role in the struggle for justice (health equity) in America. A former Service Employees International Union researcher, Jennifer provided research and strategic support for organizing and policy campaigns in Minnesota, Illinois, and Pennsylvania during her five-year tenure. Jennifer is currently pursuing a Masters in Public Policy and certificate in Health Administration and Policy at the University of Chicago.

Kelly Letzler used her culinary school education as the Executive Catering Manager for Just 'Cause Catering, the revenue-generating business of Second Helpings. Kelly started at Second Helpings as the Food Production Manager, helping the organization in its food rescue, hunger relief, and job-training program.

Noah Baker Merrill is Co-Director of Electronic Iraq's Direct Aid Initiative, which provides funds for critical medical care to Iraqis forced to flee Iraq. At the time of his interview, Noah was Program Coordinator for the American Friends Service Committee Southeastern New England Program. Noah has worked on, studied, and reported on conflicts and peacebuilding efforts in Africa, Europe, Latin America, and the Middle East.

Carmen Patrick Mohan is a Clinical Fellow in Medicine at Harvard Medical School and a resident-physician at Cambridge Hospital. She is also co-founder and former board chair of Health Students Taking Action Together (HealthSTAT) in Atlanta and a member of the board of directors of the Community Campus Partnerships for Health. At the time of her interview, she was a medical student at Emory University and the chairwoman of the Reproductive Health and Justice Committee of the Third Wave Foundation in New York.

David Neal is the co-founder and former Executive Director of the Fair Trial Initiative, an organization dedicated to improving the quality of representation received by people facing the death penalty. David is currently an attorney at Brooks, Pierce, McLendon, Humphrey & Leonard, LLP, and the Vice President of the Z. Smith Reynolds Foundation. He continues to serve on the board of directors of the Fair Trial Initiative and to represent clients on North Carolina's death row.

Elizabeth Ouzts is the State Director of Environment North Carolina, a statewide, citizen-based environmental advocacy organization. Her lobbying and policy research focuses on global warming and land conservation. After college, Elizabeth was an AmeriCorps member in Newark, NJ, completed the PIRG (Public Interest Research Group) Fellowship Program, and was the Director of NCPIRG.

Sanchia Patrick is the co-founder and board chair of Baby Peaches, an Atlanta organization that promotes healthy parenting and adequate care of infants from birth to three years. Professionally, Sanchia works as a Customer Marketing Manager for Kimberly-Clark Corporation headquartered in Roswell, Georgia. At the time of her interview, she was a Product Manager for Danish medical manufacturer Coloplast.

Mel Rodis has a small law practice in Phoenix representing primarily immigrants in a variety of civil law matters. Mel has served as the Program Manager and Staff Attorney for the Arizona League to End Regional Trafficking, representing victims of slavery, debt bondage, and indentured servitude. She also worked for the Community Legal Services Farm Worker Program representing migrant and seasonal farm workers.

Christiana Russ is a pediatrician at Boston Children's Hospital who specializes in international pediatrics. In 2007, she spent time working in an Anglican mission hospital in Kenya and will return to East Africa in 2008. Christiana is Chair of the Executive Council Standing Commission on HIV/AIDS of the Episcopal Church (USA).

Annie Sartor currently lives in San Francisco and works as an organizer at Rainforest Action Network. At the time of her interview, she was campaigning for ocean protection and ecological sustainability as the West Coast community organizer for Oceana in Santa Monica. Annie has also worked to protect immigrant rights in San Diego and volunteered in support of reproductive freedom.

Dara Custance Schulbaum uses her MSW as a therapist in a partial hospitalization program for youth with mental health and/or behavioral problems. She also leads multi-family experiential group therapy. Dara started her career as a peace education teacher in public schools and has worked on juvenile justice issues.

Araceli Simeón Luna works to strengthen civic partnerships in Latino communities as the National Parent School Partnership Director for MALDEF (Mexican American Legal Defense and Educational Fund). MALDEF, headquartered in Los Angeles, works to protect Latino civil rights through litigation, advocacy, and educational outreach.

Andrea Strimling is a scholar-practitioner whose work focuses on international peacebuilding. She served for over a decade as a Commissioner with the Federal Mediation and Conciliation Service, where she mediated disputes, taught negotiation and mediation, and worked with the US government, NGOs, and academic institutions to promote cooperation in peacebuiding. She is also a co-founder of the Alliance for Peacebuilding.

Marie Trigona lives and works in Buenos Aires, Argentina, where she participates in a direct action and video collective called Grupo Alavio. Marie has reported from Argentina for numerous progressive media outlets around the world. A writer, radio producer, and filmmaker, Marie does work that focuses on labor struggles, social movements, and human rights in Latin America.

Scilla and **Paul Wahrhaftig** have led a life that combined work and practical idealism. Paul, now retired, at different times practiced as a civil rights lawyer, worked with the American Friends Service Committee, and was a stay-at-home husband. Scilla worked for a travel company, was a stay-at-home wife, and then worked for the American Friends Service Committee.

Mackinnon Webster most recently worked with the UN Office for the Coordination of Humanitarian Affairs in Thailand and New York. She also coordinated a membership organization of Asian-led humanitarian NGOs in Malaysia, performed strategic planning for a health-related organization in India, and worked on urban public policy issues as a Coro Fellow in St. Louis. She currently is completing a Masters at the Fletcher School of Law and Diplomacy, Tufts University.

Rachel Weidenfeld worked for three years at the Justice Resource Institute (JRI) in Boston. At JRI, she helped to coordinate support services for people living with HIV/AIDS and worked in a therapeutic after-school program for children and adolescents affected by HIV. Rachel began a Masters Degree in Social Work program in the fall of 2007.

Erika Wiggins is the Ohio EPA Public Involvement Coordinator responsible for Southwest Ohio. At the time of her interview, Erika was the Outreach and Development Coordinator for Clean Fuels Ohio. Clean Fuels Ohio works to increase the use of cleaner fuels and energy-saving transportation technologies. She holds an MS in Human and Community Resource Development from Ohio State University.

Samantha Yu was the Director of Policy Analysis for the City of Los Angeles's Commission for Children, Youth and Their Families at the time of her interview. She leveraged resources and connected people and programs to ensure that her constituent groups were served by the city. She is currently a Senior Legislative Deputy for Los Angeles City Councilmember José Huizar.

Appendix 2: Interview Transcripts

We loved speaking with people about their practical idealism and are grateful for the stories they shared. The following section includes the transcripts of five interviews that we conducted in order to learn more about how people have integrated social change work into their lives. For space reasons we could only include a small fraction of the total number of interviews. More transcripts are available at www.practicalidealists.org. For authenticity's sake, we have kept them almost exactly as they were spoken with only light editing for clarity.

Interview with Josh Dorfman

Josh: What is my life like? My life is spent pretty much 24/7 building a company that makes environmentalism relevant. We're trying to build an environment-minded, lifestyle company to present people with choices that they can easily integrate into their lives. So to be very specific, we focus on very distinctive, very contemporary modern design, finding designers who are building furniture, home accessories, and bedding, using materials that are going to be better for the planet than other alternatives. By doing that we are presenting our customers with the opportunity to say, "Here are beautiful products that stand on their own merit and they also have environmental responsibility embedded in them." Given the fact that we live in a consumption-driven economy, a consumer-driven society, the actions that we take every day in our lives are to buy things, right? So given those realities, what we try and do is present a very practical solution. We say, "Here are alternatives to the actions you take in your daily life, to the things you buy." You can have an incredible lifestyle and have all the things that are important to you from an aesthetic point of view and at the same time know that your actions are making your planet cleaner and healthier and your home cleaner and healthier. That is what I do.

Alissa: Can you tell me a little bit about how you came to be doing this?

Josh: I can tell you a lot about it. I'll give you the highlights and I think it applies to a number of your questions. I have always been somebody who wanted to do work that was going to be meaningful to me. Now meaningful to me was not always about the environment. My values, or what's been priority in terms of my values, have shifted over time.

A year after I graduated from college I went to China and spent a couple of years living in Nanjing. Actually, as soon as I graduated from college I went skiing in Vail for a year and was a ski bum. I had three or four different jobs and skied five days a week, which was fantastic because that was my top value at the time. My top value was, you know, powder and deep snow.

I was raised in a family that stressed an understanding of current events, politics, and international events. My mom's background was pretty international, just in terms of her education and graduate work and things she had done. That had always been emphasized. I studied in France my junior year, in Lyon, and had a great experience. I lived with a family and was really immersed into that culture in a way that I hadn't experienced before. So the path I went down and the choices I made after college can probably be traced back to that experience in France of living with a family and being involved in their life.

It was a very working-class family so you got to see how French people really lived. Lyon is not a very touristy city so it's real French life and that was a major experience for me. I came back to college for my senior year and was writing my thesis. This was 1993 so the Cold War had ended relatively recently; the Berlin wall had come down just a few years before. Tony Lake was the national security advisor for President Clinton and he was going around giving a lot of speeches saying that the next major country that we would have to deal with would be China. So I was searching for a senior thesis and got very into this idea that China was going to be the next major world power that the US would have to confront. I think as Americans we do well defining ourselves as a nation when there's someone to define ourselves against. We know we're good when someone else is potentially bad.

So in my senior year I wrote a thesis on China and that's what led me to go. I went thinking I'd have a career in diplomacy and it would be good to spend a couple of years and learn the language. I was teaching at a university. I would say for people who want an international career, the best way that I've seen to go overseas is to go teach. Right out of college, you don't necessarily need a background in order to get hired into a paying job. You can go and actually be abroad.

This was China 1995. It was kind of like the Wild West in terms of economic development and the possibilities for entrepreneurship. It was still a stifled society but there were more and more opportunities. Three weeks into teaching, I randomly got a job working for a company called Kryptonite that makes bike locks. They had just moved their manufacturing facility to Nanjing serendipitously, and needed someone just to be in that factory once in a while. They wanted just to show that there was someone there watching what was going on. So that's the job I got hired into part-time. At first, it was an opportunity for me to continue to develop cross-cultural skills. How do you work in a business environment? How do you understand Chinese concepts of face? Dealing with elders in that society, just maneuvering through elements of the Chinese cultural setting was a fascinating thing. So, that part-time job quickly took on its own momentum because it was a country that was rapidly developing.

We were selling bicycle locks mostly to the United States. And I went to Kryptonite and said, "Look, there's a billion people riding bicycles in China; I think the opportunity is here in China." So without having a business background, without that being part of how I was raised, I got the OK from headquarters back in the States. I took my student who spoke the best English and she became my assistant and off we went to Nanjing and started selling bicycle locks. We stumbled onto some very large accounts randomly and this experience took on its own momentum. Six months later I was opening an office for Kryptonite in China and was becoming their chief representative and traveled around the country.

Alissa: It's all about taking initiative.

Josh: It's all about taking initiative. So I stayed in China for almost two years. Definitely by far the most profound experience I've had—personally, growth wise, just being exposed to the other side of the world and an entirely different way of living. And after two years I needed to come back to the States and more than anything else just kind of reintegrate myself. I was really embedded in Chinese culture sort of like in France. I wasn't in Shanghai or Beijing or Hong Kong where it was much more cosmopolitan or with an expat community. This was Nanjing. My whole life was Chinese; my friends were Chinese; everyone I worked with was Chinese.

Alissa: And you're thinking, "Am I Chinese?"

Josh: Yes. When you're overseas in a situation like that you can, over time, lose sight of who you are. You're growing, but at the same time that bedrock of how you were raised and who you are sometimes gets murky. And it was starting to get murky for me. I realized it was time to come back to the United States.

So I came back to the States. This was '97 and I was trying to process the experience I'd had in China and trying to figure out what to do next back in the States. I wasn't sure that I wanted to go back overseas but I was starting to think of myself as a very internationally minded person and as a professional. And it was around this time, as I processed my experience, that I also became really interested in economic development. I started thinking about the World Bank and the IMF and the Washington Consensus and the kinds of policy that we were espousing all over the world. Having been on the ground in a culture for a couple years, I asked myself, "Do these prescriptions make sense in reality? Yeah, they make sense in America, but are they right for another culture?"

At that point I decided to go back to business school as a way to use the experience that I'd had, which had been fascinating. But I hadn't really been steeped in what I called business fundamentals. I was very entrepreneurial: let's run around the country and try and negotiate deals and figure out what we can do. I kind of wanted to take that experience and ground it in an MBA so that I would be more well rounded. I thought I wanted to go back to China and help companies go to China and that would be kind of the role that I would play. So diplomacy was kind of put on the sidelines. I was also thinking about what was happening with globalization and feeling that economics and business were really driving the world. I felt that politics was taking a backseat to these forces that were incredibly powerful and I didn't think that was necessarily a good thing. And then in '98, when I was in business school, we had the Asian financial crisis and I really started thinking a lot about the role for business. What is positive? What is not positive? And I started thinking more about my experience in China. I started to realize that here I'd been there trying to sell bicycle locks to a billion Chinese where at some point in our lifetime, probably sooner than later, that same billion—a billion plus—were all going to be driving cars. And when a billion Chinese people are driving cars, that means that there will be five more United States of car drivers on this planet. And that's impossible. It's impossible. You talk about unsustainable! It's like disaster and it's a coming reality. It's going to happen. For me, that was my environmental epiphany.

So I came to focus on the environment not from any sort of wilderness sentimentality or to keep the water clean or to save the pandas or stuff like that. I think that is good and important but it wasn't my background. For me it was just: "Here's a major problem and I'm going down this path of business and I enjoy what I'm doing but I cannot go take some job that I feel will be doing damage in the long run." So then it became a question of asking how I was going to move forward. My values shifted from a focus on the international to trying to figure out how to align these things so I could still lead the kind of lifestyle that I wanted. I didn't necessarily have to choose to go work for a nonprofit that is mission based in order to do something that's about my values. Working for a nonprofit wasn't a choice I wanted to make. I did not want to sacrifice the kind of lifestyle that I'd like to be able to provide for myself and who knows, as I go down the road here, my family.

Alissa: So there you are. You have graduated from Thunderbird and you're like, "Here I am back in the world with people again. What do I do?"

Josh: Well it wasn't so straightforward. I subscribe very much to the idea that you just have to try everything that makes sense to you. I was twenty-six when I went to Thunderbird and in my mind I was telling myself I wanted to go do this China stuff. I also knew deep down—at least for the time—that I was done with China. But I didn't know what else to do. So it was a period of struggle, real internal struggle trying to figure out what it is that's going to do it for me. It was uncomfortable, really uncomfortable.

I took an internship after two semesters and went to Hong Kong. I did go back and I was working for a group called the Economist Intelligence Unit, which is part of the same parent company that puts out *The Economist* magazine. This is sort of their political risk consultancy. And I was doing work in Hong Kong, analyzing for different clients the business market in China or healthcare in Asia, and I just found that I didn't really want to be there. The international thing that I had decided was my identity wasn't really resonating anymore with what I wanted to do. There was real conflict.

In business school I was dating this girl who lived in Germany. We met out at Thunderbird in Phoenix. I went to Hong Kong; she went back to Germany. This was part of the whole process here. We actually broke up at this point but I was still totally in love with her and wasn't really willing to let that go. Thunderbird has a campus in Geneva, and one of the things I did think about, going into business school, was that I wanted to come out of business school speaking Chinese and French. I felt that it would put me in a really strong position. So I went to Thunderbird's campus in Geneva. Here I was in business school and I really had no idea what I wanted to do! So I went to work for an auto parts company in Paris called Delphi Auto Systems, which was part of General Motors. It had just been spun off. I got this job working in production control and logistics. And most of my friends were like, "Why would you possibly want to do that?" I was like, "No, it's like strategy, it's like logistics, it's like where things go." They were like, "No, it's terrible." So I sort of set out to prove them wrong and I thought it would be fun. It was really boring and not fun but I learned a ton. And, of course I was in Paris, at this big multinational global company. I learned a ton about how these companies work, what they do well, what is totally dysfunctional. I learned a ton about supply-chain management; I learned a ton about things that are so helpful to what I do now.

I came back to the States to finish up at Thunderbird. I'd been away for about 15 months with internships and studying overseas. It was 1999 and we were right in the middle of the dot-com boom and all that crazy stuff going on. I didn't even know it was going on because I had been out of the country. I came back and my brother picked me up at the airport. We're driving back to my folks' place looking at all these billboards. I was like, "What is going on?" I'm very drawn to big ideas so I was like, "All right, I need to go work for a dot-com. I need to get involved in this." So I finished my last semester and got a job working for a start-up company in Los Angeles. It was very dot-com-y. They hired me without a resume and I was on a plane to London two weeks later. It was great. Nobody had any idea what was going on. I was working for this internet startup and it had the potential to be a great idea. There was this genius who was going to make it all happen. Well, that didn't happen. Six months later I quit.

I felt that this company wasn't being managed in a way that resonated with my values. In fact it conflicted with my values. We didn't have a product. I was being asked to use a lot of my Thunderbird contacts overseas to set up appointments and promise things that I didn't think we could deliver. So ultimately I left. It was September 2000 and I sort of fabricated a life crisis. I wasn't really having one, but I really wanted to go to Montana. So I quit my job and I had this vision that I would go to Montana, get like a guitar and a fishing rod and go down to the Black River and get a case of beer and hang out and figure out my life. So I got in my car, drove to Montana and went to a pawnshop, bought a fishing rod, a guitar, and a "guitar for dummies" book, because I actually don't play the guitar. And [I also bought] a case of beer and checked into a motel and was like, "All right, the plan is about to go into action." So I woke up the next day and there were about eight inches of snow on the ground. This was in Missoula. And I thought, "All right that plan is done with but let me start in on this beer and see where we get." So I ended up that afternoon in a bookstore. Until that point in my life, I was a very big reader. Authors were my heroes: John Irving, Hemingway. They were a heavy influence in my travels overseas. So I was walking through the bookstore and I found the section on screenwriting. I love movies and I was like, "All right, I live in LA; authors are my heroes. I'm drunk and I'm a pretty good writer. I'm going to write a screenplay. That's what I'm going to do." I went back to LA and started writing a screenplay based on my experience in China.

This is sort of a very LA story. We were in Santa Monica. The guy who lived next to me was a big fitness guru or trying to bill himself as a fitness guru. He was constantly trying to sell me vitamins and various other things. He knew that I just quit my job. I had told him I was now going to become a screenwriter, six months after getting my MBA and having $100,000 in student loans. So he said, "I have this job proposition for you." For close to a year, I would write for about three or four hours a day and then for the rest of the day we were engaging in eBay arbitrage. We would scour the papers and buy up all the used fitness equipment that people were just getting rid of—Soloflex, Bowflex, Universal Gym, you name it. I would drive out, pick it up in my little Honda and come back and post it on eBay and sell the stuff all over the country. And that's how we made our money. My friends from business school would visit and they'd open the door and there'd be like ten Soloflexes in my apartment and a Universal Gym in the kitchen.

Alissa: And you were like, "I'm keeping fit."

Josh: Exactly. They'd be like, "Josh, I really think..." They'd have these sit-downs, you know, like an intervention. "I really think there's a place for you in the corporate world; just come back."

Alissa: So how did you transition out of that?

Josh: I wrote a couple screenplays that were great to write. I would say that I now definitely draw upon that experience, understanding how to craft a message, to craft a story. I have tremendous respect for it. But it again felt like that really wasn't the path for me. I still didn't know what the path was for me. I felt again like I needed to come back to New York and just figure some things out. LA was cool, but it wasn't really a great place for me personally. So after about a year and a half, I came back to New York and once again I had no idea what I was going to do. I was dating a girl at the time. We went out to Boston for the weekend and we were talking about a PhD program in international relations and some of the things I'd been so into thinking about in college. I guess I'd had this idea in the back of my mind, probably all through my twenties. I'd had this idea to become a professor; get a PhD and be able to work in international organizations and have that kind of life and lifestyle, including consulting. So I applied to PhD programs because I thought, "I'm about to turn thirty and if I don't go for my PhD at thirty, it's never going to happen."

I applied to PhD programs and was living at home. This was a little bit tough to take because I'd lived all over the world and done some pretty cool things. And now I'm like twenty-nine, about to turn thirty, and living at home. So I applied to PhD programs. I decided that if I was going to be this academic for the rest of my life that I really needed to have some hard-core skill. So I applied for a job as a carpenter's helper so I would know how to fix things. I went to interview for that. I didn't really know how I was going to interview for it. The guy I was interviewing with was like, "Yeah, your resume doesn't really..."

Alissa: ...scream "carpenter's helper."

Josh: He was like, "What do you know about carpentry?" I didn't know anything about carpentry. It had said carpenter's helper/driver. So I was like, "Well, I'm a really good driver and I know about Sheetrock." And he said, "Well that's not really going to cut it but we are opening a second office. Why don't you go over there and run it for a few months." They were like a rent-a-handyman for the day type business. So I spent eight months pretty much fudging my way through estimates in people's homes and learned a lot about crown molding and stuff like that. It was really cool.

There has always been this theme that has pervaded everything I've done. I have started things without having any idea what I was doing. And there's something about that that draws me to experiences that are going to be totally new. In some ways there's the potential there to be consistently setting yourself up for failure because you really don't know anything about it; but on the other hand, it's fun, it's exciting, it's new. So I did that for eight months and I got into a PhD program in political science at George Washington University. So I went down to DC.

I had put up a website called addressglobalization.com, where I was pulling together all of these links for the things that had been circulating in my mind about politics, economics, and the environment. I was interested in how these three areas were interacting on a global scale and what that meant for human civilization. I thought I wanted to do research and went into this PhD program for a semester. I did fine but I realized that I actually had no tolerance to be back in academia. So this PhD program wasn't really going to work out. It was going to be four, five, or six years until I was actually done with it. I was sitting in a class one night, it was the January of the second semester, and we were reading a book called something like *Rulers of the World*. It was a political economy textbook that I didn't understand. We're in this little classroom; it's like eight o'clock at night; it's winter. And I'm just thinking, "You know what, I don't care who rules the world and I don't care about this book." It just felt so abstract to me.

I think I really needed that academic program to help me solidify what I understood the world to be and what I felt were the issues and the challenges that needed to be addressed. It was sort of therapeutic in some ways. It was kind of like the world was this giant psychoanalytic environment for me. I became more confident in what I believed. Here is what I came up with. I believed the world is messed up, that business is doing things that are harmful, that government has a role to play but I don't want to play that role. I want to work with people who are making change happen in a very action-oriented, tangible way.

I started working on a business plan for a new venture. It eventually became Vivavi. This was about three years ago. I started thinking that there were companies out there that I could work with using my business background to help market them to find customers for products that were environmentally responsible and, for lack of a better word, cool. I was not thinking of hippie, burlap sack type stuff but a real product. So I started doing a lot of research and informed my professors that I was having a family emergency and wouldn't be coming into class for the rest of the semester.

I wrote this business plan and started searching for companies that had this kind of product. It took about eight months to pull this business plan together but after about three months into the semester, I informed them that I wasn't coming to class. I made the decision that I was going to pursue this business.

That wasn't an exhilarating moment. That was a really scary moment. I knew that I had synthesized ten years of interesting experience and internal struggle. I had had a relatively privileged upper-middle-class upbringing in Westchester County where opportunity is very open to you. Sure, there is responsibility because of that but all those kinds of things came together. It was just clear to me that here is a path that just felt like the path that I was meant to go down. This was just what I was meant to do. When I knew that I was leaving the program and going to do this, it was like one of the most frightening weeks of my life. That first week I thought: "Oh my God, all right, I am doing this thing." It was this fear (and almost this paralysis) that made me realize that if I don't wake up today, pick up the phone, and call ten companies, this isn't going to happen. There was no one else involved. It was either going to happen because I was going to make it happen or it just wasn't. There weren't excuses; it was just really stark and raw. That's it, either you're going to go do everything that needs to get done and try to figure it out or that's the end of it, there is nothing.

Alissa: Did you have second thoughts? Did you think: "It scares me but it really, really has to happen"?

Josh: It was more like that. "It scares me but it has to happen." I felt that it was really the right thing to do. So there weren't really other alternatives but that didn't make it easier.

Alissa: How did people in your community respond? Your parents and your friends?

Josh: My parents were awesome. They have definitely been through some shocks with me...

Alissa: "I'm in Montana."

Josh: Yeah, exactly: "I'm in Montana, I quit my job. I'm going to be a screenwriter." Even, "I'm going to China." But they took a look at the business plan. I was mindful that these were my decisions that I was making but they're still my folks and I wanted their support, their emotional support. And they were really cool. They thought it sounded pretty sound. My folks are also entrepreneurs. They run a sleep-away camp for kids up in New Hampshire. It's a family business; it's pretty cool. So they were supportive.

With my friends, it is hard to know. When you do things that are beyond other people's comfort zones, the responses are generally awkward to begin with. You're like interpreting silences when you tell someone that this is what you're doing. And that silence might be like, "Wow, that's incredible." When you tell someone that you're going to start this company or do this thing, you sometimes see something register on their face that isn't making them feel comfortable. What they're thinking is like, "I could never do that, or I should quit my job?" They just immediately go into their own head. It's never really about you. I wouldn't say that my friends were majorly supportive. When every step you are taking is challenging the status quo you get messages like, "Why don't you just go to law school?" Or, "Why don't you just go get a job on Wall Street?" Then they'd be much more comfortable with you because they could relate to you.

Alissa: Has this been a rewarding decision for you? How is it going?

Josh: The very short answer is that it is incredibly rewarding. It gets more and more rewarding. It certainly is more and more rewarding financially. But way more than that, it is the feeling of influence. I know that people look at Vivavi and what we've been able to build. If they're a designer they're saying, "Wow, that is an outlet where I can sell my product. That's what I'm all about." If they're a customer, they're saying one of two things: "I've been looking for this," or, "I didn't even know these things were possible." Six months ago I started hosting a radio show as an outgrowth of the company. I host a radio show called *The Lazy Environmentalist*. It is on Sirius Satellite Radio. It's fun to go into the studio and be able to bring designers and entrepreneurs and other people who are really active in pushing these kinds of options and making them available to a mainstream audience. And we are doing it in a way that feels very relevant to me—environmental choices that are about the way we live. To be able to help those people get their message out there and to be in a position to really feel like you're influencing the debate, that's incredibly rewarding.

Alissa: What about on the flip side? Things that are hard about it or that have negatively impacted your life?

Josh: For me personally, I've spent three years married to this company. There are sacrifices. I mean I could have gone and done something else and made a lot more money, but I know for myself I would have really wanted to leave the whole time unless it were really about my values and what I believe in. Beyond that, it can be lonely. You want things to go really fast and they're not going fast. When people aren't responding to your message and to what you're putting out there, you take it personally. Everything that this company stands for is me. It's my values that I'm putting out there.

When I first launched the company, I thought my friends would race to get to our website and find some cool products. I thought, "Yeah, my friends will buy some products, be supportive, my family will buy some products," but that did not happen. And it can be lonely being an entrepreneur. People who aren't entrepreneurs don't have much of a sense of what it's like. So my two or three other friends who have started companies, we commiserate a lot. We understand each other.

Luckily my immediate family was very supportive even though my dad still couldn't understand why my mom's handbags were like $300 each.

Alissa: Have you been able to pay off your loans?

Josh: I'm paying off my loans; I'm not in deferment. Like I said, financially it's a challenge. You live with a lot of stress. There is a lot of responsibility and that definitely can cause a ton of stress.

Alissa: Even though it is stressful, would you recommend this type of work to others?

Josh: I'd say absolutely. I think that it's absolutely worth it. It's 100% worth it. It's so rewarding; it's really so rewarding. It's so rewarding also to see a vision realized.

Do you know Hunter S. Thompson? He worked for *Rolling Stone* for a while. He was a crazy, crazy dude. He had a quote. I'll probably get it wrong but it was something like, "You don't find men with small imaginations on top of tall mountains." If you have vision and you have imagination, if there is this thing that is important to you and you want to see it actualized and it is part of your personality, then I would say absolutely go for it. I would say too that if you get to the point where you're swimming and you're out in the middle of the lake, you can either keep going or turn back. It's the same distance both ways. You have to be the kind of person who is always in the middle of the lake and you're always going to keep going because there's so many points where you would still really rather turn back.

Alissa: Is there anything else that you want to share?

Josh: I certainly have advice for people who are thinking through their own paths. I have some practical advice. People have written about this and it's a little bit trite, I guess. I do think we are living in a world where obviously people change jobs a lot. Companies don't show loyalty; you have to perform and if you don't perform you're gone. Even if you are performing, you might be gone. I think that the best way to deal with that is that everybody is their own brand. We are constantly marketing ourselves as our brand and I think that the internet creates possibilities to build your brand so that you become known for whatever it is you believe in. I think that everybody should have a blog. Whatever is of interest to them, they should write about it. With search engines when someone is searching Google, they're going to find you. At some point they're going to find you. And if you're becoming known for something or expressing an interest in something, then you're going to connect with people who are either going to want to employ you, buy your product, or collaborate with you. There's such an opportunity there. If you don't do it, you're not going to be seen or heard. That's just the world that we're living in.

My path has been very swerving, nonlinear, but I believe that everything does work out and you learn from every experience. Pursuing what you believe to be your passion I think always works out. When I was in this PhD program, there was a Japanese guy who could have continued through the program or taken an opportunity to join the UN. He had come to the PhD program to ultimately join the UN but he had the chance to join right away. That is what he really wanted to do. We were talking about it and he asked, "What do you think?" I said, "Well I think it's obvious: you should go join the UN now." He was like, "Well, what about the credentials?" I said to him, "You just have no idea what's around the corner anyway, what life holds in store. You should go with what you want to do." That's so much more true now than ever before. I think it's always about doing what you're passionate about and that will lead to the next opportunity.

Interview with James Forman, Jr.

James: I am a professor at Georgetown Law School. I'm also the founder and board chair of the Maya Angelou Public Charter School here in DC.

I still remember the first line of my law school application and now that I've read law school applications I realize that a third of them start the same way. I wrote that my interest in law school grew out of my commitment to social change. When I went to law school I was going to be a civil rights lawyer. I remember in the very beginning of law school we had to envision that it was ten years after graduation and we had to give ourselves an award. This was such a classic Yale Law School thing, like you are so great that you need to think about the award you're going to get after graduation. Anyway, I chose the Thurgood Marshall civil rights award. I didn't know exactly what kind of civil rights work I was going to do. The traditional pattern was that you could do education or employment discrimination work. You could also do housing discrimination or voting rights work. I knew I was going to do something along those lines.

The summer after my first year of law school I worked for the NAACP Legal Defense Fund in New York. I got assigned to work with the death penalty unit. I had never thought particularly about capital punishment and the death penalty. I worked with an attorney named Steve Hawkins who is still very active in the field. It was a really incredible and powerful summer for me. It helped me to think of death penalty work as civil rights work, but I still didn't think of the criminal justice system specifically as civil rights work. Now there is a substantial focus on the civil rights implications of the criminal justice system: how many poor people and people of color are incarcerated. But if you can believe it, in 1989 criminal justice was just beginning to be on the radar screen. The war on drugs is really what drove the incarceration rates to what they are now and that was just beginning. So, for example, the NAACP Legal Defense Fund didn't have a criminal justice unit. The only criminal justice work they did at the time was death penalty work and that was understood as being a civil rights issue. The broader issue of incarceration of black people, brown people, poor people, was not on the radar screen of the established civil rights groups. It was just getting there.

Later, I went to work as a law clerk. I worked for a judge in Los Angeles, William Norris. Then I clerked on the Supreme Court for Justice O'Connor. It was while clerking that I really saw the absolute tragedy or travesty that is indigent defense representation at the trial level. The legal representation that people get when they are poor, they are charged with a crime, and they face trial is the biggest scandal of the criminal justice system. Everything else, to me, pales in comparison to the fact that we have so few quality lawyers [as public defenders] and we pay them so little. The results are what we see—a lot of people who don't get due process. So I thought, "Well, I better go and be a public defender. That is what I was complaining about so let me put myself on the front lines and do that."

The lawyers I had worked with at the NAACP were my mentors: Steve Hawkins in the New York office did death penalty work; Steven Bright runs the Southern Center for Human Rights in Atlanta, a death penalty organization; Bryan Stevenson in Alabama; Janell Byrd, an NAACP legal defense lawyer in Washington, DC. These lawyers were the people I had worked with or had worked for and had gotten to know. When I told them I wanted to do trial work they all thought it was a great idea. They all mostly handled appeals. They were therefore well aware of the problem at the trial level. They were very supportive.

It was a hard decision for me because when I was in law school my dad was diagnosed with colon cancer. My dad, who was very active in the civil rights movement himself, never had a lot of money. It's hard as a kid to see either one of your parents struggle financially, economically, or with their health. My dad was struggling in all three of those domains. I remember specifically when I was clerking at the Supreme Court, that the big law firms were paying $50,000 signing bonuses. So on top of your regular salary, if you were a Supreme Court clerk, you got a $50,000 signing bonus. I remember thinking really hard that year about whether I wanted to go work for a law firm because my dad could have used the money. If I did that, that would put me in a position to be able to support him in a real way over time. You know, I talked to him and he said, "You should do what it is that you want to do and you should follow your heart." I knew that he had done that. He had given up his job as a schoolteacher in Chicago, which was a secure middle-class job for a black man in that era. He had left it to go join the civil rights movement in Atlanta. I knew, both from his words and also from what he did at my age, what he wanted me to do. I ultimately didn't go to a law firm and decided to go join the public defender's office in DC.

Alissa: How was that experience for you?

James: That was incredible on a lot of levels. The DC public defender's office is really the premier public defender's office in the country. It was set up as a model public defender's office in the late 1960s. Because of the quality of people it attracted and the political support to keep its caseloads at a reasonable level, it's been able to maintain a standard of quality that a lot of places don't see. To be surrounded by the most incredible bunch of lawyers that I've ever worked with, to this day, was an amazing experience. My mom came and visited. She said, after walking through our offices, she felt that it was like a movement office. She was talking about the civil rights movement. We were in the basement of this old decrepit building and it was battered and nasty and no one wanted to be down there. Everyone had political posters up and it was a real sense of us against the world. Nobody really cared about our clients other than us and that is hard. It is stressful. At the same time you develop a sense of mission and a sense of community—a sense of purpose that just keeps you going. You don't even think about the long hours because you're so passionate about what it is that you're doing. And that, I think, was an amazing job to have out of law school.

I always tell my students now that I think students make the mistake of picking a job they're not passionate about to start with. They have the idea that they will get a job that they are passionate about later. That is actually the opposite way that people should go about thinking about it. In law there's so much cynicism, there's so much of a sense that you're not really making a contribution. If you don't experience a job that you're passionate about early on, you might not ever know what it can be. You don't know what it can feel like to have that. You never have that bar for yourself. You don't actually know until you're fifty, when you have a mid-life crisis, what you've been missing, and then, a lot of times, it's too late. Based on my experience, my big advice to all of my students is to start with the thing that you're passionate about and then you'll at least know what that feels like. Later on you can decide if you want to give some of that up for something else. For me, working as a public defender in DC was the greatest decision I ever made and it was the greatest job I ever had. I did it for six years.

Alissa: In a sense, it sounds like choosing meaning over money.

James: Sure. When I started I made $28,000 a year. This was in 1994. It was twelve years ago but still not that much money. So I made less than I had made as a law clerk. As a law clerk we made something in the thirties, I can't remember. I had student loans and all that, but once I passed the bar, my salary went up to something in the low to mid-thirties. I talk to my students about how you can actually pay off your debt while having a low paying job. Nobody believes me. I sit down with them and go over housing expenses; I talk to them about having a roommate; I talk to them about not having a car. We do budgets. I tell them that the number one thing you have to do to make it is that whenever you get a raise, because even in public defender jobs you do get raises, you take half of your raise and add that to your loan repayment. You never see it, you do monthly automatic withdrawals so you never see the money. But you can't be a martyr; you have to get some extra money. You take half and give it to the loan company and take half and give it to yourself. If you're disciplined about it you can pay off your loans.

Alissa: That was a beautiful thing to say.

James: For the first year and a half, at that time, I mostly represented juvenile clients. A lot of it is social work, about finding placements and programs for kids. The judges don't want to lock the kids up, for the most part. If you can find a program that seems like it's going to meet the needs of your client and you can get your client in it, the judges, at least in DC, typically will give your client a shot at that.

I realized that we had this incredible batch of highly trained, aggressive, committed lawyers all running around the city trying to find the perfect program for kids. The problem was that there weren't enough good programs. There were more good lawyers than there were good programs for those good lawyers to find. I thought about that and I asked myself what I could do about it. I started to talk to my clients about, "What would work for you?" They didn't want to get locked up, but they also didn't like the options that they had. I started talking to educators as well about what they thought would really work.

David Domenici and I started an after-school tutoring and job-training program for kids. David, who was a lawyer at a law firm at that time, bought this little tiny pizza shop on the corner of Florida and North Capital. We incorporated this little nonprofit and we had six kids. They were clients from the public defender's office. The deal was, they wanted to work and they wanted to get paid. So we said, "OK fine, we'll hire you at this pizza shop but you have to come and be tutored by us in the afternoon." We had a tutoring program and a small business. We tried to link up the academic content of the tutoring program to the business. We taught English by writing up press releases for the business. We taught math by doing the accounting to run the business. It was a great program but it was insufficient.

The kids that we were working with were in the worst schools. A lot of them had been kicked out of the regular schools and were in the alternative schools. The regular schools often have enough issues, but the alternative schools were really terrible. And so we said, "Let's try to start our own school." We went to the district first, the DC public schools, to try to see if we could work out an arrangement, but the bureaucracy at that time was unable to deal with it. It was such a weird proposal. At about that time, the charter school law passed, which allowed us to apply to be a charter school. We opened the first year as a private school that was free and supported by foundation grants. In our second year we became a charter school.

I took a leave from the public defender's office to go and start that school. I did it for a year. David and I were co-principals and taught classes. We had twenty kids, five teachers, a counselor, and a little row house. We worked from eight in the morning until eleven at night.

I worked full-time at the school for a year, then I went back to the public defender's office. Ever since then I have been a five- to twenty-five-hour a week volunteer at the school. It depends on what's going on that week and what they need me to do.

Alissa: How were you able to fit both of those things into your life?

James: It is hard; it is hard. I'm not going to lie. There are some times you feel stretched and pulled. There are times when you feel guilt about not attending to other parts of your life beyond that. It has certainly made relationships challenging.

When I think of what I did, it was a lot of external relations: a lot of making connections, fundraisers, a lot of trying to meet with people and then putting them in touch with somebody at the school. Sometimes it was meeting with someone from a company to try and get them to hire our kids as interns. Other times it was meeting with a group of people to try to convince them to go and work as tutors at the school. As the chair of the board I used to have a lot of governance responsibility, a lot of fundraising responsibility. I also, at times, have taught classes. I'm getting ready to teach, actually, a mock trial elective class that will be in the spring semester.

Alissa: Who helped you? Was there someone who helped you develop a sense of what was needed in terms of external relations and fundraising?

James: A lot of it we made up as we went along. If you're passionate about your product and you have basic communication skills and a willingness to work hard, you can sell it. And that's basically what we are. We're passionate about our school; we're passionate about our mission; we're passionate about the fact that what's really distinctive about our school is that we have very high standards for our kids. No one else in the juvenile justice system does. Most programs for kids that are at risk have standards that are incredibly low. You go into juvenile court and the judges tell kids, "Don't get re-arrested; don't use drugs." I mean what kind of standard is that?

Most people aren't trying to work with the kids who are so far behind and I understand that. In some respects it makes the schools harder to run. It can bring your test scores down if you're actually recruiting kids who have low test scores. There are structural obstacles as to why this is hard for people, but that is the reality. So we're bringing the high standard movement from education together with the juvenile justice system. These kids really need a lot of help and we're passionate about that. We think that that's absolutely connected to the civil rights struggle. David, my partner, likes to quote Martin Luther King, Jr. King talked about how this work is hard as crucible steel and that's exactly right. It is hard. But if you're passionate about it and you're willing to talk to people about it and if you have the results to back you up, then in my opinion you don't need that much training. The technical stuff of fundraising is 10% of the game. You can learn that 10% but you have to have the other 90%.

Alissa: What about your transition to Georgetown?

James: I've always loved to teach. When I was in college I taught at Exploration Summer Program. That is a program for high school kids, at that time run out of Wellesley College. Now it is run out of Yale. I did that for three summers. I also taught LSAT prep to college students when I was in law school. When I left college, I went back to Atlanta, where I'm from, and went back to my high school to try and get hired as a teacher but I didn't have the proper certifications.

I've always loved teaching and I've always been interested in writing. I've always had two parts of me. I've had a part that's academic: out of college I almost went to get my PhD in history instead of going to law school. I've also been practical, wanting to be engaged in the world. Being a law professor is a lovely place because law, of all of the academic subjects, is probably the one that's most naturally engaged with the world. Law is policy, and policy is how our courts work, how schools work, and how regulations actually affect people's lives. Government structures and legal regimes affect people's behaviors in the world. So law can be really closely tied to the things that I'm also interested in.

Alissa: Is that what swayed you away from doing something like a PhD in history?

James: I had two TAs at Brown who were both getting their PhDs. They both said, you know, you should beware; this is a long hard road. I ended up thinking that I could make more of a direct impact by going to law school. I went to Yale, a very academic law school, which trains a disproportionate number of law professors in the country. Ever since law school I've thought about teaching. Every year I would talk to my mentors at Yale and say that maybe I would go into teaching this year. But I loved what I was doing so much! A lot of my mentors said, "Well wait; there will be a time that's right for you." That right time was a couple of years ago.

Alissa: How did you decide that it was time for...?

James: You know I hope one of the themes that comes out of your book is that life is an evolving process. I think, sometimes when people go back in time, they like to re-create a conversion and feel that there was this moment of transformation. Sometimes that's true for people and I guess at times that's been true for me. I think, in this case, it was more just an evolution. It was always something I had thought about doing. It just happened. I don't have a great turning point for that.

Alissa: OK. So did you just apply for the job at Georgetown? How did it happen?

James: I left the public defender's office because I had a disagreement with the management in the office at that time. It was just time for me to leave. I was then looking around and trying to figure out what I was going to do next. A journalist, who I had gotten to know because she had come to write a story about Maya Angelou, was at the time at a place called the New America Foundation. It is a think tank that tries to recruit budding public intellectuals. So she said, "Why don't you apply for a fellowship at New America?" I met with the head of the New America Foundation, a wonderful guy named Ted Halsted. I got a fellowship with them. I just sort of bumped into that opportunity. The fellowship gave me space to begin to do some writing and to think about some of the policy issues that I had been involved in. I could now step back from them and take the time to write.

I then contacted Jeff Lehmann, a professor at Michigan Law School, who I had known for some time. He would call me every year and say, "Are you interested in teaching at Michigan?" Over the years he became a tenured professor, and then he became the dean. When I was at the New America Foundation I called him up and said, "You know Jeff, we've been talking for like eight years. Well, I think I want to try this." And he gave me very good counsel. He said, "Unless you're really ready to totally commit to being a law professor then you probably shouldn't go for a tenure track position. You should probably go for a part-time, visiting/adjunct type position." And because he was the dean, he could basically snap his fingers and make it happen at Michigan. So I started teaching at Michigan while living in Washington. I would fly to Ann Arbor every week, I would teach a couple of seminars, and I would come back to DC. I enjoyed that enough that then I decided to actually try to get a full-time tenure track position. I went on the job market and interviewed at a bunch of places and ended up at Georgetown.

Alissa: Is there anything that you wish you had done differently or that you might change if you were to go back and do it again?

James: The one thing I definitely wish I had done differently was in college. It took me a while to figure out what I was going to major in. At the end of my sophomore year I decided to major in history. I remember sitting down with my advisor when I had two years to go. There were three things I wanted to do: I wanted to study abroad in Brazil, I wanted to write an honors thesis in history, and I wanted to get my teaching certification. She looked at all the credits I needed and she said you can only do two out of the three. You don't have enough time left to do all three of those things. And I made the mistake of picking writing the honors thesis and going to Brazil. Now Brazil was the right decision. I would have been a lot better off doing the teaching certification rather than the honors thesis. That was right before Teach For America started and at the time there wasn't a mechanism to teach as an uncertified person. That was a mistake. Once I graduated I could have gone home to Atlanta and gotten a teaching job. Maybe I would have eventually gone to law school anyway; but it would have been a more meaningful experience after college to go and do that.

Interview with Nicole Hoagland

Nicole: I am the youth programs director at Time Out. We're a very small organization. It's just my executive director Mette and me. She does everything and I do everything else! As youth programs director, obviously, I'm most heavily involved with the youth. We have a youth support group that meets every week here in Charlotte. We also have two satellite groups that meet in Hickory and Gastonia. Those groups are facilitated by volunteers. I'm kind of over them, making sure that everything is cool.

We have an emergency housing program for youth who have been kicked out of their homes because their parents or guardians find out about their gender identity or sexual orientation. I'm the one who has structured that program. The program, for the most part, rests on the backs of our volunteers. Our volunteers are the ones who open up their homes for varying periods of time to allow youth to stay there. I'm the emergency contact for that program. I'm also there all the time making sure everything is cool and that the transition into the home and eventually the transition out of the home is successful. We also have social events for youth so that folks aren't feeling that being gay is so very difficult all of the time. This should just be a really fun place for folks to hang out and develop friendships and relationships. We do a lot of fun things—everything from camping overnight to hiking up a local hill, picnicking, midnight bowling...just fun things for folks to do. A lot of those ideas come from the youth. The midnight bowling is actually a new thing. We've had folks say, "Hey, I'm a bowler, and I want to do that!"

We also have a youth leadership team called the Youth Programs Committee. Those are youth who are most interested in being leaders within the organization. They take the lead in organizing fundraising efforts for the organization. They also are in charge of organizing larger social events. We just got done doing our annual talent show and we'll have an awards ceremony in August. They do those kinds of things. I'm there as well as volunteers to help motivate them and increase their leadership capacity. It is tough work! Tough work but lots of fun!

Alissa: What are some of the things that you like the most about your work?

Nicole: I love the youth the most. One of the other programs that I oversee is a speaker's bureau program. Youth are trained to go out into the community and speak about what it's like to be LGBT or an ally. I find myself in every single speaking engagement incredibly empowered and inspired by their strength and their ability to communicate their experience and infuse all of these consciousness-raising messages into the audience. They inspire me. I think this work is really about building relationships with the youth and seeing them grow and watching their relationships develop with each other and the adults that we bring on board. By far, the youth are the best part.

Alissa: What are the things that are challenging or not quite the best part?

Nicole: I think being in the South is a challenge. It's very difficult to be down here. I would guess that a lot of us who are doing this work feel a certain responsibility to do the work here because somebody has to. But, oh, wouldn't it be nice to be somewhere else and have the work be just a little easier because you have broader community support. Mette and I, just this past weekend, received an email from some religious fanatic who has been emailing us, telling us that we're going to hell and we need to be saved by Christ. It's that kind of thing.

It's not even like, "I don't know about LGBT issues." It's that broader religion, "you're going to hell, burning in hell forever and ever and ever unless you repent," sort of stuff!

Alissa: And you are based in a church.

Nicole: Interesting, isn't it? Although Charlotte is a particularly difficult region of the country to be "out" and LGBTQ, particularly because of the South's traditionally conservative religious beliefs, we are also fortunate to have incredibly supportive houses of worship in our community. Holy Trinity Lutheran Church is just one of several in Charlotte. However, OSA is here: Operation Save America. The organizer lives right in Concord, which is the city directly north of us. OSA has been very active in Charlotte Pride Day, really destroying the climate and environment that we want to create for the community for just one day! One, out of 365! So that's a challenge. Being a small organization is really a challenge. To have two folks pull off what we pull off is exhausting. Incredible, but exhausting, absolutely exhausting. Those are the two things that I can think of off the top of my head.

Alissa: Let's take a step back and talk about what you were thinking about as you were transitioning out of undergrad.

Nicole: I graduated with a degree in psychology. I didn't really know what I wanted to do but I knew very basically that I wanted to be involved with the community and infuse some of the energy and politics that I had into the community. I had always liked youth but didn't necessarily focus my efforts there. I graduated knowing that I wasn't going to be able to do much with a degree from undergrad. The goal was to go to grad school. I didn't get into grad school straight after college so I ended up working in a co-ed group home. I loved the work but most of the folks around me didn't have education and energy. I just felt like, "What are you doing here?" They didn't have what I felt kids in the system needed. These kids needed to be encouraged and empowered. Yes, they needed structure and discipline, but I felt there was too much of the negativity and not enough of the "I'm going to build you up." "Yes, your life has been crappy up until now but by God your future is wide open."

Alissa: So was this for people who were wards of the state?

Nicole: Exactly. The first group home I worked in was for folks diagnosed with Willie M, which was a category as a result of a class action suit. It was basically kids with emotional problems. Classic stuff. In fact, that category doesn't even exist anymore. I jumped around a little bit from here to there, just waiting to get into school. I got into school a year later and I landed a job with a battered women's shelter at the same time that I started school. I did a part-time program. It had been a while since I had felt the click [of being at a place that really felt right]. It was a phenomenal organization. It was called CVAN [Cabarrus Victims Assistance Network]. It's in Concord [NC] and run by an absolutely incredible woman, Mary Margaret Flynn. I feel like I need to get down on my knees every time I see her. She is phenomenal, brilliant, and any skill that you would hope somebody would have as a person, as a friend, as an executive director, she had it. She was phenomenal.

I spent five years there working on the crisis line and working with women at the shelter. It was also during that time that I did a teen program. I was going into high schools, talking about dating violence and date rape and loved it! It spoke to me, similarly as my work with battered women, but it spoke to me in a different kind of way. With youth I can be my funky crazy self and they're like, "You're kind of crazy, but I like that." With adults, they are kind of like, "I don't really know how to take that." I always felt more comfortable with youth because I could just be myself. I left CVAN after five years. It was a very, very, very, very difficult decision. It was tumultuous for the last six months I was there.

Alissa: How did you make that decision?

Nicole: I was really struggling. I loved the women that I worked with. I loved the work that I did. I still felt connected to it. The politics were important to me. But I also wasn't being fed in the same way that I had been fed there. It was really confusing to me because a lot of the folks there had worked there for a long time, like ten, twelve, fifteen, seventeen years. I had only been there for five, and I'm like, "What's wrong with *me* that I can't continue to do this work? Why is it that I don't feel connected?" During those six months my executive director and I sat down on numerous occasions. In the end she said, "You know what, Nicole, it's just time to move on. You've done your work here, and you've done what you can do here and it's time to move on." I realized at the same time that although I loved my work, there wasn't a lot of upward mobility. I didn't really think of myself as a "moving up the ladder" kind of person but I wasn't being challenged. Although the crisis line always offered the opportunity for something new and unexpected, it was still the same sort of thing. I found that I really needed to go somewhere else. I needed to be challenged a little bit more.

I left there and ended up working in another group home! I figured with an MSW, things would be different. It's a different organization. I'm in a different position. It's going to be much better. But it so wasn't! It was horrible. It was horrible. It was not that the work was horrible, because I loved working with the kids. It was my first management position so it was a challenge for me working with the staff. For the most part I loved the work that I did. Unfortunately, the structure around me was crappy and I did not get any support. When I'm doing crisis work with youth who are in crisis because they are having behavioral, emotional, and medical problems, I need support around me. It just wasn't there.

I left there and I said, "You know what, I'm done with North Carolina." I had never expected to be here this long. I grew up in New Jersey and went to school in New York for undergrad. I loved Ithaca, loved Ithaca, loved Ithaca! It's a phenomenal city. I was like, "I'm just done. I've done my time here. I'm done. I'm just done." I went to Portland, Maine. Loved it. It had been a while since I had been in a city that had spoken to me. I landed a job and was literally packing my stuff and bidding adieu to North Carolina when I sat down with one of my friends who had been talking with the previous youth program director in this organization. And I said, "Tell me a little bit about Time

Out. What are they looking for?" And he said, "They are looking for someone from within the community with an MSW and two years' post-grad experience." I was excited but also slamming my head against the wall at the same time because I was so close, so close! I interviewed here and I just love it here. I just feel so lucky to be working with youth and working with youth within my community. Mette is phenomenal. You know, in a small organization, again, there is that risk of not having a structure around me. Again, working with crisis and working with lots of issues, I need something that I can fall back on. She has just been a blessing to me, and I would never say that if I hadn't been doing this kind of work this long. I feel so lucky to have her here. In moments of pinch, and there are plenty, she is readily available and that's necessary for me. I don't know if it's necessary for anybody else, but it is necessary for me.

Alissa: Can you talk a little bit more about the role of mentors in your path?

Nicole: I feel really lucky to have had several women in my life who have provided mentorship. Probably the first woman that I can remember—at least the first woman I'll give credit to, which probably isn't fair—was a professor in my undergrad, Carla Golden. She just knocked me off of my seat. I literally would sit waiting in the classroom for her to come in. I'm a little weird. She was phenomenal! Anything that I thought I knew, she would just be like *boop*, "Well, you know, I'm not necessarily saying it's not true but think about it. Think about it." I was just like a puppy dog; she was just unbelievable, unbelievable. I've been in contact with her recently. We email back and forth every now and then. Phenomenal.

Another woman, Judy Jackson, was someone I worked with at the suicide prevention and crisis hot line up in Ithaca. I was privileged enough to meet a woman there who again was just full of warmth and grace and knowledge. She had an ability to just mold somebody into who you know they're going to be. Just gently mold them. Again, she was just brilliant. I am so grateful to have had all of the knowledge that she has passed on to me. And then again Mary Margaret at CVAN and

Mette. I have been very lucky! I haven't even sought them out; they've just kind of, by chance, come to me. I'm so lucky.

Alissa: Why do you think you struck out on this path?

Nicole: I don't know. I think I've always been moved by injustice whether it was something as small as an injustice in my house, between my mother and me, or an injustice in grade school. I just always felt moved by something that I felt wasn't functioning well. I've also felt moved to be available to folks who don't feel like there's any support available, who are just so isolated and feel like their experience is so *theirs* and nobody else has ever experienced anything like that. I think injustice and being available to folks is what speaks to me.

Alissa: How have your family and community responded to the kind of work you're doing?

Nicole: My parents, although my mother more so, have always thought that I was a little kooky. They haven't been unsupportive but haven't particularly been supportive of the social work field. Although I should say that they paid for my undergraduate education and paid for my graduate education. In that sense they are very supportive. They are upper middle class and I think they are worried about financial struggles. My mom was an activist in her early years but I think that my being in a small, gay organization in North Carolina is a bit too much for her. You know, they say that they're proud. It's a mixed bag with them. Most of my friends are actually social workers or working for social justice so I'm pretty in tune with them.

Alissa: Can you talk about ways that you have been impacted positively or negatively by your career choice?

Nicole: I feel fed. I feel fed. What I did know very clearly in my undergraduate is that I didn't want to be one of those people waking up every morning dragging heels and saying, "I don't want to go to work." I made a pact with myself that I would not be that person. I am pleased to say that I'm not. I look forward to going to work now. Some days are more exciting than others but I don't drag my heels. I get out at least as much energy as I put in.

My father sat down with me many months ago and said, "You need to think about retirement and money and dadada, dadada, dadada." He just went on and on. "You're not making any money and dadada." My mother at the same time walked over to me and gave me an article in the newspaper about a former youth who had come to Time Out. It talked about how before coming to Time Out Youth he had tried to commit suicide twice and after coming here had found a community of friends and was doing really well. He had just blossomed into this incredibly compassionate, capable individual living in this world. And I looked at him [my father], and said, "Not for one million dollars would I change the feeling that I just got from reading that article." There is no money that's worth that. There's just not. The twelve- to fourteen- to eighteen-hour days are worth it. There is nothing more valuable than the feeling I just got from that. That's the positive stuff.

The negative aspect isn't necessarily about the profession; it's more about me as a person. I feel lucky enough to feel like who I am as a person and who I am as a professional are intermixed. That's a great feeling. But what also tends to happen is that I have a hard time separating them. It requires extra effort to create a social life and to be as committed to that as to the work that I do. That's a challenge. It's a mixed bag. Every job has its own thing and so I get this, and I don't get that. I just can't imagine doing anything different.

Alissa: Do you have any advice for folks who are thinking about getting a job? Is there a trade-off between meaning and money?

Nicole: I think it's a really personal choice. Clearly, we all have to survive. There are bills that we have to pay. For me, the right answer was finding my passion and figuring out where I could put that into the community. But I've also been allowed to lean on a previous partner who helped to support me. If I get in a pinch, I know I could call upon my parents. I have made some sacrifices, but I know, in the end, that if something really dramatic happens, I have some people I could fall back on.

Alissa: Have you been OK for the most part?

Nicole: Definitely, definitely. Can I buy the new car and get the latest whatever? No. But is that what's important in your life? I think folks just need to sit down and figure out what's going to be important. Because if you go down the path of finding your passion, chances are that you're not going to have the money. So what's going to be valuable to you? My mom exclaimed, "You don't even have cable TV! You don't have a computer." She makes me out to be a pauper. But I have a computer at work and food in the fridge. You've just got to find out what's most important for you. You need to recognize that there will be sacrifices. But, if you go for the money, there will be sacrifices there, too. It's just what's most important for you.

Alissa: In terms of your career and your life, what are some of the changes that you hope that you are helping to bring forth in the world?

Nicole: I think it is relationship development. I think it's that pebble in the water theory. Even if there's only one person whom I've touched, they hopefully go out and touch people similarly. I don't even need to really *see* the fruits of that labor. I feel the fruits of that labor. I don't even necessarily have a goal to change people's perspective. I think my philosophy is similar to my college professor's. She wasn't like, "You're wrong!" She just kind of tipped me off my chair and said, "Think about it." In the end, that's what I hope that I'm providing folks. Just take one step back from what you think that you know and what you have been taught. Just consider whether that's something that you want to embrace for the rest of your life. Is that a truth that you want to embrace?

Alissa: Are there things that you would say to somebody who wanted to work for social justice or social change?

Nicole: One thing that has been really effective when I've been training folks to be on the speakers bureau panel and they're freaking out is telling them, "This is your life. Value your experiences. They are so valid. There is nothing that you can say that would be wrong." Just affirm people's experiences. Do the classic social worker action of meeting people where they are. If you decide you want to go into social justice work, what do you want to get out of that? How do you see your life developing? So you're a social worker, what are you doing with that? No matter how hard we all try, we can't be perfect. As painful as it is, it is okay to make mistakes. Some of the biggest mistakes I've made have been some of the most generous learning experiences that I've had. I'm different from my mother who would say, "I've had these learning experiences. I don't want you to have them." I think it's important for folks to experience their own shortcomings or mistakes and learn from them. Remember, I'm different than you, I have a different way of going about things so what worked for you or didn't work for you may or may not work for me. I'm going to try it anyway, damn it!

Interview with Jennifer Jordan

Jennifer: I'm a research analyst at Service Employees International Union (SEIU). I do research for hospital organizing campaigns. On paper my job description can cover anything from doing contract costing to help with bargaining. For example, there might be a unit in a hospital that needs to negotiate their first contract or renegotiate existing contracts. There's a lot of use of spreadsheets and math to determine whether the hospital has money and, if so, how they can allocate it towards wages, healthcare benefits, or retirement benefits. The stuff that I have mostly been working on is organizing. There are places where we don't represent the workers and the workers are trying to organize. My work tends to be more of a corporate campaign model where we try to do things to leverage the employer so the workers have enough support and enough coverage to be able to organize. Right now, in the labor environment, it's more than just saying that you want a union. It takes a little assistance to actually get from the place where you're thinking that you want a union to the place where you have one.

I went to Macalester College and I majored in political science with a strong minor in history, and most of that was labor history. The summer between my junior and senior years in college I did an internship in DC with a governmental affairs firm. I helped them lobby anywhere from small pharmaceutical companies to different state organizations on lots of different issues. I loved it; I enjoyed my time on the Hill. I really enjoyed the firm that I was working with, Smith, Dawson & Andrews. It was very small and I got to do a lot of really awesome work.

It was funny because I got the job because a family friend had put me in touch with them. They have interns come out every once in a while so the office wasn't set up for an intern, which I think was the best thing that could have happened for me. They hadn't decided to give me busy work. It was pretty much a combination of "do these things that we actually need to get done," like help represent clients, and "go to whatever hearings you're interested in and write them all up." I did a lot of writing, a lot of correspondence with their clients, and I really liked it. I knew that I was going to come back to DC after I graduated and I was thinking that I wanted to do some kind of lobby-related work.

In between my summer out here and graduating, Bush won his first election. Oh sorry, Bush became President; so it was a little different by the time I made it out here. My mother told me on election night in 2000, she was like, "Jennifer, you need to go to grad school, you'll never find a job in this market." It felt like that when I got back to DC. Organizations that I was interested in working with weren't hiring. Then the week after I got out here there was 9/11 so things were sort of crazy. I didn't want anything to do with Capitol Hill, and in DC it's really hard to end up doing anything governmental affairs–related unless you have Hill experience and know people there but I couldn't stomach the Hill culture.

I tried to explore direct service opportunities in DC, which is a really really small section of what people are doing here. Everything is so governmental and governmental affairs–related. I ended up spending, I guess it was eleven months, working for the nation's capital Girl Scouts Council. My mom was very involved in Girl Scouts and I had grown up in the organization and they were hiring when I was out here. What I did for them was community outreach in Latino and low-income neighborhoods north of DC in P.G. [Prince George] County, which I was excited about when I took the job. (As I foreshadow the rest of the experience.) I like the organization, I think it's great. There's enough money within the Girl Scout organization that if a group of young girls decides they want to do something, they can actually make it happen financially. It's wonderful.

What I found not wonderful was working with the volunteers. A major part of the organization is the volunteers; they actually carry out the programs. They are what make Girl Scouting happen. The volunteers I worked with needed a little bit more to do with their lives and I found it very challenging to manage volunteers effectively. It was a really good experience for me because part of what I learned about myself and my work style is that I like to know what's on my desk before I come to work that day. It helps me feel like I'm accomplishing things. It helps with anxiety and all sorts of stuff. After doing that for a year and not finding the fit that I wanted, I started to job search. One of the first places that I applied to—one out of three places that I ended up applying to—was the SEIU for the labor research position that I'm in today. It's funny, I didn't interview at any of the other places I applied. I went into my interview at SEIU with the bare minimum background of what the union was doing but an understanding of labor unions that was based historically. My grandpa is in a union but labor isn't really a part of my reality so it was definitely kind of a shot in the dark in a big way.

My first interview wasn't actually an interview. It was a writing test and a skill set test. It was the first time that I had seen numbers in two years. It was all this quantitative analysis and I was like, "I love this, numbers are really exciting." It's interesting how, when you get into this history and nonprofit world/path you don't really use numbers anymore. It's a lot of writing, it's a lot of qualitative work and not very much of it is very quantitative. So I was definitely excited to see that, even on paper. I was interested in the job for those sorts of reasons.

Alissa: So would you suggest that people keep numbers alive, even peripherally?

Jennifer: Yeah. I don't know that they die. I think that what happens is that you get out of practice of seeing them and using them so it becomes scary and you think, "I can't do that." I also feel like I used to write it off as what the right does. "Oh they use this funny math," but it's useful to be able to do the same sort of thing.

Alissa: When you made that transition into this job, were there people who helped you on the sidelines and supported you?

Jennifer: Definitely. One of my professors at Macalester, who taught most of my labor history courses, was definitely a support—a supporter during the transition. I talked to Peter Rachleff a lot about what I was doing. He was definitely excited about me being at SEIU and he knew some ex-Macalester students, some graduates, who had also ended up in the union so then I reached out to that network and talked to them, too.

I think a lot of getting a job is timing. The job market in DC is such where there are tons of positions open but the time frame in which people respond to you is just really sporadic. So I could have done a lot of different interviews before I ended up at SEIU but I don't know that any of them would have been the fit that I found there and the sort of challenge that I found there. I like the fact that there really is a skill set and expectations that are kind of hard. I like being able to measure my progress against those elements. I don't know that that's always so easy to find in a nonprofit sort of organization.

I didn't really talk to anyone about my decision [to take the job with SEIU]. I talked to my parents, I guess. I feel like, had I had broader conversations with family members, people in Illinois that I'd known, I would have been more aware of how pervasive the stigma is about the labor movement, among some communities. Since then, going home, I heard the sentiment that it was a bunch of union fat cat talk and labor unions hadn't ever done anything for black people. It's funny because now I'm very much rooted in this and I feel like I have ammunition to, maybe not argue against those sorts of ideas, but be in conversation with them. Had I known people's feelings from the start, I think it would have made me a little more hesitant. I do think that SEIU is a different sort of union and other unions are more traditional.

Whether in reality or just in rhetoric I find that SEIU is a little bit more willing to be more of a movement, and a broader movement, than just labor and economic issues. SEIU had a statement against the war when it first started and it has passed resolutions like supporting same-sex marriage. It's done a lot of stuff that I think traditional unions don't do and don't feel that they need to do so it makes it a really exciting place to be a staff member. I think that SEIU's politics line up with mine fairly well, as good a fit as I think I'd find. And the labor component means that it's not just about politics in an intellectual way. There are small wins every month, every year, that really mean something. It's not like on the policy level where, "Oh, we can fight a policy battle forever." Now I know that people take home higher paychecks [because of the work I helped to do] and that is very exciting.

Alissa: You found out, when you got home, that people had different opinions about labor—were there other reactions from friends?

Jennifer: At the time, none of my peer group in DC worked with the union so I think that there was just an understanding that those jobs were hard to get. I feel like that's because you have to take a test before the interview but also because of the whole tradition of nepotism within the labor community. It can be hard to get in.

Alissa: What do you think brought you to this kind of work? Tell me your philanthropic autobiography.

Jennifer: I don't think what I'm doing is at all removed from my family's values even though my parents aren't union members, aren't active union members. Definitely, economic justice has been a large part of what my family works towards. For those reasons, it might be surprising that I ended up in a labor union but it's not surprising that I'm working on the issues that I'm working on.

I'm trying to be involved in some faith-based organizing with the Catholic Church that I'm a member of here. We were having a little meeting and talking about "where did your values come from?" I was thinking, "Oh, my parents had one bumper sticker all of my life." It was a Catholic campaign for human development sticker: "If you want peace, work for justice." I thought, "Oh, I guess it was written, right there on the bumper sticker, and I've never really stopped to think about what that meant." You know, it's only been one. It never changed. It was never an election bumper sticker, it was just that one.

Alissa: Tell me a little bit about how the choice to do this labor work has affected your life.

Jennifer: I just think that it's definitely not only shaped my work life but my social life. There are a ton of labor people in DC and I feel like my social circle is very full of people who are also involved in the labor movement. One of the most exciting things that I've done in the last four years was that I spent three months in Minnesota working on the campaign in '04, the election in '04, rather. I was able to do so, still keeping my job in DC because SEIU put a lot of money into America Coming Together. I went to Minnesota, which was great because that's where I went to college and it was nice to be back in a community that I knew. I canvassed for three months. It was exciting to canvass for the election. It was exciting to canvass not for Kerry but as an anti-Bush let's talk about issues sort of thing. Prior to the '04 elections, I thought that what could swing an election or what could bring out progressive voters or make people who were on the fence into more progressive voters was conversations about the issues. I've since changed that idea but at the time it was what I thought would work and it was very exciting to try to make that happen.

Alissa: What changed your mind?

Jennifer: I think that I thought it could be a quick process. Maybe I haven't changed my mind wholly, that it's about conversations, but I think they happen over a longer period of time: years instead of just months before the election. I now understand how deep [rooted] everything is. It's very deep.

One of the best experiences during that time was working alongside members of SEIU because both members and staff got to go out to the field. To be with people from New York who were experiencing Minnesota in the fall for the first time—people who would normally talk to their coworkers in the building that they're cleaning together—door-knocking about something as important as a national election was really amazing. It was an excellent opportunity for me to work alongside people that I would probably never have gotten a chance to work with otherwise. And I think that that's really huge. You know, you get into this path where the cross-section of society that you're really going to interact with in any sort of meaningful way gets really small. It was a great opportunity to just challenge my assumptions and work with a very, very diverse group of people.

Alissa: What does it mean to you to find meaning in your work?

Jennifer: I think that it's the wins that I've been involved in—the contracts, the new organizing, going from a market where the pay is $5.50 an hour and seeing that increase, stuff like that. It's also the opportunities to be able to step up and do even more challenging work. I think that there is a definite understanding that human resources are really huge right now in the labor movement. There's a lot of stuff to do. There's a lot of room for people to step up and take on more responsibility.

The rewarding part is knowing that I'm doing important work every day. I think that there are times when I totally lose that. Part of that is being in DC and feeling so removed from the stuff I'm actually working on. Like the campaigns that I'm working on have been in Illinois, Minnesota, and Pennsylvania. So part of my move to Pennsylvania is to actually work at the local level and work in the state that I'm living in.

Alissa: Has your work had any negative effects on your life? How about work-life balance?

Jennifer: I think that there are times where I overwork but that's only because I care about the product and that matters. Part of the DC culture is that things go in spurts. Because you are removed [from events happening at the local level], you'll have a lot of work for a second and then things go away. If you were to talk to me a year from now hopefully I can say that I've found something very healthy to do to keep my life very balanced.

Alissa: The financial effects of this choice, like loans, financial security or insecurity...?

Jennifer: I am very financially secure. I'm also a member of a union that isn't SEIU so I have a union salary, wages, benefits, and vacation time. It's been a really amazing thing in my life.

Alissa: What's the change that you'd love to see at the end of this journey?

Jennifer: I don't know what it looks like. I think that part of what made me so excited about labor work is that I think that money is huge. The difference in making an additional $2 an hour is really, really huge. It means access to a lot of things. So I would love the end result of this work to be people organized to get what they deserve for the work that they do: work actually being valued.

Alissa: Would you recommend this kind of work to other people?

Jennifer: I would. I think that it's great. Absolutely would! I think that part of what has led me to such a positive outlook about the work that I do is that I came in doing research. I think that right now one of the easiest ways to enter the labor movement is through organizing. If you were to ask an organizer all of these questions, their answers would be a lot more intense. I think that organizing is amazingly rewarding because you are talking to people and making connections with workers every day but the burnout factor is really severe. I've watched a lot of people who should be in the labor movement leave because they got burned out in organizing. I would encourage whoever was interested in doing labor stuff not to come in through organizing or to understand that the whole movement isn't just the way that organizers are treated in the movement.

I'm not an expert on this but I think that the organizing departments of most major unions are the holdouts in the old labor mentality. It's people who have been there the longest and see the labor movement or the culture of the labor movement as something that is static. It's the place where you are exposed to more harassment, more intolerance, and all of those things that the labor movement is trying to change. It's really intense. The understanding is, if you can't cut it, you can't cut it...or you don't care enough to be able to cut it. And how do you complain about a sixty- or seventy-hour workweek when the people you're working for are working so many hours?

In the end, organizing is about empowerment, so my understanding is that when you're working a seventy-hour workweek, you're not empowering anyone. At some point you're working too much and the people who you're working with aren't working. There's got to be a balance of people who want the union owning and participating in the work so you're not doing it all by yourself.

Alissa: Is there anything that I haven't asked you that you'd like to share or thoughts about making this transition or even about what you're going to do in the future...?

Jennifer: I think that my path has been more defined than it would have been had I done anything else. I feel like I haven't gone to grad school because I've been able to do meaningful work without another degree. Part of that is that there is tons of stuff for me to do out there. It's not a matter of "Oh, I'll get bored because there's nowhere to move, there are no more responsibilities"—no, that's not the reality. So I think that, instead of grad school being the place where I prep for my career, it's kind of now the place where I go when I get burned out, which could be ten years from now...or five. And I think the part of moving to the field, to Pennsylvania, for me is seeing what work is really out there and then making my decisions after that. I think that it's irritating to my parents because they have been pushing grad school, since 2000, and I've chosen to do other stuff.

I do think that the labor movement and SEIU is a place where I can do anything I want to do without going to grad school. If I wanted to come back and do more policy work, it's an amazing place to do policy work. Not only would I be able to support and push policy that I believed in but the membership of millions and millions of people would be in my network. It's like the biggest grassroots network you could ever want to have. It's also a great place to do communications work, if I ever wanted to do communications.

Alissa: It's an organization where there's mobility and you can express all the different skills that you have.

Jennifer: Yes. And refine them in a very practical sort of way. So yeah, grad school has definitely become the place where I go when I can't cut it anymore, I'm tired, and I want to do something new. I think that my grad school future has moved from policy and applied programs to, oh, urban studies or labor history. I'm tired of actually using education to…I want to write for other people who would like to read what I write.

[After the major taping was over]

Alissa: You were talking about that transition between the Girl Scouts and the union.

Jennifer: Yeah, wanting to quit my job and feeling the need to tell my mother every day that I hate this, I hate what I'm doing, and she was emphatic that I couldn't quit until I found another job, so I took some time off and applied and did whatever. More than just the logistics of that, I felt like it was one of the first places I had a huge disconnect with my mom. I think that her understanding of a job is that a job is what pays you. You're lucky if you like it. And I was like, "I know I have to do something I like every day." I think that it's really interesting: the differences in how people approach work and what they're looking for.

Alissa: So what do you think is that relationship between meaning—having a job that's meaningful to you—and having a job to make money? How do you think about weighing those—you know, balances? It sounds like on her end, your mother was like, "You have a job to make money. You need to pay off your bills and do all this stuff." And on your end you were like, "I need a job that's meaningful to me." How do you explain that or reconcile that to other people, or...?

Jennifer: I don't know. I don't think that I will ever be able to reconcile that to my parents. I feel that it's very—it's a learned sort of value. I don't know that it necessarily came from my household. It came more from my socialization in college. I think that it's peer specific, you know. There are places where you go off to college and you know you're going to make money, that becomes the meaning of what you work for. My friends from school are all trying to find jobs that they actually care about and want to do on a day to day basis.

Interview with Samantha Yu

Samantha: I work for the City of Los Angeles Commission for Children, Youth, and Their Families. I'm the director of policy analysis. My work generally involves data collection and presentation for use by policymakers. This department was created ten years ago. It came out of a recommendation from a committee that Mayor Richard Reardon created. It is to be a focal point within the city to coordinate the work of various city departments working for children, youth, and their families. At that point we had a large number of programs administered by a number of different departments that were not communicating with each other. This department was created as a sort of clearinghouse of information and also to be the leader and facilitator of collaborations and partnerships. A lot of my work involves connecting people to other programs that they may not be aware of, convening and facilitating meetings between different departments and agencies, and finding ways to leverage resources.

What I like about my job is that you can really see some direct impact on program administration, even at the community level.

Looking at the people who went through the public policy program with me, I understand that it's exciting that I have this opportunity to do very concrete policy work straight out of school. I'm getting to meet a lot of terrific people who have a great store of knowledge, who know very much how the city works, and who have worked for many years to change how the city works. It's a really interesting time particularly with our new mayoral administration. For a couple of years we really felt like we weren't getting our message through. I think that the new administration has brought in a direction that's very much in line with what we are trying to do.

Alissa: What about some of the things that are not as wonderful?

Samantha: I would have to say that if there is something that I don't enjoy that much about my job, it's the number crunching. I don't have to do a lot of number crunching, but I do have to do some. The data that comes into our office goes through me, and then I farm it out to other people, aggregated into different geographic areas, whatever the case may be. I do some number crunching and manipulation in order to prepare briefs. I'm not a numbers person, never was, and I don't think I ever will be. I need to change that though.

We get a lot of data from the County of Los Angeles, which collects the majority of data in this area. We get data from the Census Bureau. We also get data from the Los Angeles Unified School District [LAUSD]. In each case it really involves working with people to get the data by the city boundaries, by the administrative boundaries of the city. No one really collects data by the administrative boundaries of the city. We have to translate the data into our sectors. That's something I have to work through that I don't enjoy.

Alissa: If we could take a step back for a second, take me to undergrad and what you were thinking at the time.

Samantha: I did my undergraduate work at the University of California, Berkeley. I did my bachelors in political science. I had always been interested in doing a humanities degree. I can't remember the rationale as to why I went into political science. I was considering history and English, but I ended up going into political science. I really thought that I would go into something more academic, more theory based. The first two or three years of my undergrad career, I really thought that I would go on and seek a masters or potentially a doctorate in political science. It was something that interested me a lot. I really enjoyed the classes, the professors, and the like.

While in college I took a job with the City of Los Angeles in the mayor's office. I was working in the intergovernmental relations office helping out with whatever was necessary. It was really interesting to see how an official's office worked. It made me think, "Well, do I really want to go into theory or do I want to go into something more hands-on?"

After I graduated I took a job with this department. This department is an interesting mix. When I came on board, it was around the time that our current ED was kind of changing the direction of the department, making a link between the community work and the policy work. He was trying to find a way to bring the two branches more closely together because they used to operate rather independently. I also got a chance to dabble in issues such as childcare and public health. At that time, I began thinking that policy work would be a really interesting option. I could use the theory but also get into the hands-on part of it. At that point I was beginning to think, "Ok, I really think that I'd like to pursue public policy." I tend to make snap decisions and at that moment I thought, "Ok, I'll fill out an application for a public policy degree." That was where I ended up concentrating my applications. I did do some applications for political science degrees in political theory but I really focused on policy-related programs.

I graduated from undergrad in December and I went back to school in August. I had about eight months where I was working full-time in internships. The city is big, but it's also a small community, when you think about it. I had met a lot of people so I had a lot of referrals. I had a couple of choices when I was thinking about public policy. It was either to go back to Berkeley to the Goldman School, go to USC, or go out to Georgetown. These possible choices made me think "Do I want to do state politics, local politics, or national politics?" I thought about it a lot and I have to say my decision to stay in local politics was probably more personal than professional. My family is based in this area, and I don't think I'm ready for DC yet. I thought about going to UC Berkeley, but I had just moved back to LA, and I wasn't sure I wanted to move yet again. At that point I was more interested in getting my feet wet in LA politics.

I came back to USC. I maintained my job here at the Commission and I also ended up taking a job with the Los Angeles Unified [School District]. I was working with both of them at the same time. In my second year of the masters program, I was doing both. That was really interesting. I'm really glad I did it. I was working for a board member. Again, that was an elected official's office, but it was very different from the mayor's office. The board has a really different role and a very different type of public visibility. It is much less visible. The work that they do is on a different scale sometimes. It also gave me an opportunity to connect with a lot of folks in the district, which is very helpful now. I continue to see a lot of them.

When I graduated from the policy program, there were a couple of options. They were LAUSD, the City, or going out to the GAO [Government Accounting Office] in Washington. Again, that choice sort of made itself, again for financial and personal reasons. Of course, I would love to do the GAO job. It would be a great job, but I'm not sure I want to go out to DC and do that at this stage. It was also interesting because when I interviewed for the GAO, I interviewed with the education team. When they offered me a position, it was with their homeland security team. It was really, really strange. I guess there was a panel of people and one of them was on the homeland security team. To be honest, I had not expected an offer from the homeland security team. With other teams my experience might fit. In homeland security, I virtually have no experience.

So, it came down to LAUSD and the City. That was actually a tough decision because I had a personal relationship with both. I chose not to go with LAUSD because of its bureaucratic culture. I know that sounds sort of strange because the City is also this huge bureaucracy, but LAUSD is just huge. Also, my board member at LAUSD happened to be running for City Council at that time. He was the front runner so I knew that he would be transitioning within a couple of months. Now he's actually on the City Council. So I see him here in City Hall! At that point I was thinking, "Do I want to get into a political campaign?" You have to make those types of decisions with these positions. And, of course, when they bring in someone new they'd wipe out the entire staff. At that stage, I wasn't ready to do a campaign. So I made the decision to come to the City, and I've been here full-time since July of last year. It's been almost a year now. Sort of scary! It's gone by so fast!

Alissa: You mentioned having a good chance to meet different people in the internships you were doing. Were there people who acted as mentors to you?

Samantha: My current supervisors, my ED and my assistant executive director, have really been true mentors for me. Even when I was a student, they were giving me the opportunity to go with them to meet people and see different aspects of the City bureaucracy. I have a lot of friends who have done internships in the City and they've had a different experience. I've had the opportunity to take charge of certain projects that otherwise might not be entrusted to a student. I had this opportunity because the department was small.

Alissa: Sometimes it's good to work in a very small department.

Samantha: It's a really, really small department! So, to get that opportunity as a student! Then when I started full-time, I was already at least halfway in. It was really, really good for me.

Alissa: Why do you think that you struck out in this direction? Has community service been an ethos in your family?

Samantha: That is *the* question—a soul-searching question. How did I really come this way? I had never been interested in technical fields. It has never been my forte. That's actually my family's big strength. They are very much involved in technical fields: engineering, chemical engineering. On both sides of the family, it's big. I happen to be the one that was not good with numbers. They never made a whole lot of sense to me. I knew that I loved to read a lot, write a lot. That's why for many years I thought I would do English. Then, there are a lot of people telling you, "What are you really going to do with an English degree?" And I said, "I don't know! I have no idea." I also had a very keen interest in history and politics, hence, my interest in the poli sci degree.

In terms of taking a career in public policy, I do have an uncle who currently works for the Department of Transportation here in California. Unconsciously he motivated me to think that public service was a good thing. In Chinese culture it's not always necessarily accepted. Growing up in a Chinese family, public service was sort of like, well, it's a government job. They hold all the classic stereotypes of government workers. I don't think I'm ever going to cure them of that no matter what we do. My uncle was one of those folks who, after he got an engineering degree, could have gone into the public sector or private sector. The private would've been a lot more lucrative. But he just really loved what he did for CalTrans.

I don't know how much you know about California, but CalTrans is sort of the scapegoat for everything around here, especially in LA where traffic is just horrendous. As long as CalTrans is around we will be forever complaining about traffic and maintenance and all that kind of stuff. But he's been there for almost thirty years now. It's driven him to be a better professional. He's very proud of the work he does, even if it doesn't pay the same as his peers might be paid. I've never really envisioned life in the private sector to be honest. It just never occurred to me. The nonprofit sector I've considered but not as much. I just always kind of assumed I would be here. Until recently, public policy has always been public sector–focused. I think now they are beginning to open some avenues for private industry as well as the nonprofit sector. But I always thought that for me the public sector was going to be where I wanted to go.

Alissa: You mentioned your uncle. How has your family reacted to your career choice?

Samantha: They've ultimately been supportive but they raised a lot of practical questions that were valuable. I really had to ask myself about my value structure in order to answer those questions. It was like, "What are you really going to do? Is that going to be enough for you, in terms of your financial security? Is that really practical for you to pursue that field? How long do you think you can stay in the field?" I think that these concerns really come out of an immigrant mentality. I was born here, but my parents' generation, all of them immigrated here. Their mentality is understandably a little bit different. To them life was about putting down their stakes, being able to establish themselves. I have the luxury of being established, in a sense. I'm comfortable enough to have some choices. To me, there's a cultural bias towards the technical field in the Chinese culture. I think it's more highly valued. And because of the language barrier, that became a little more engrained for immigrants; they really pursued technical fields because they could make their mark there.

I think the only humanities-based field that most Chinese families would be okay with would be law. Unfortunately for me I was never interested in going into law. I can't say why. I don't have some aversion to the law. It just never interested me. I was sort of perplexing to them. Well, if you're going into politics, law is a natural next step. But I don't think so! They raised a lot of questions: "If you take that job, you know that your salary is inevitably going to be limited. You will have to make do with that, and you'll have to adjust your lifestyle for that. Are you ready to do that?" I have asked myself a lot of those questions. I think ultimately for me, I'm comfortable with the decision at this point. I tell them that I may not be comfortable later on. But I'm at that stage in my life where I'm single; I don't have a lot of responsibilities on my plate and I feel like I can explore this option. They were in a different position. The decision was right for me; it probably would not have been right for them.

Alissa: Do you think it will be okay in the future? When you look into the future...

Samantha: I honestly think that I'll be okay. I always tell people, if I had wanted to make money I never would've gone into this field. You know that from day one. You were never going to believe that you were going to be the highest-paid person out there. But I did a career panel at USC last year with Dr. Moody. And one of his students asked, "When you are in the public sector, how do you make ends meet?" And I sort of laughed at the question. Because you know, it's not that bad! They don't pay us that much, but they don't starve us.

Understandably, I make less money than some of my friends who went into the private sector. But I told them what makes it worthwhile is that I love my job. I look forward to going into the office every day and I look forward to the work that I do. As much as I might be irritated while doing it, ultimately I enjoy it. So I said, for me, that makes it worth it. It's not that I have to make a huge adjustment to my lifestyle for the salary. I grew up in a very typical middle-class family. My salary will support that. It's not as tough as it might appear.

Alissa: How do you talk to people who are graduating and thinking about having a job, meaning versus money?

Samantha: You really just have to assess what's meaningful to you and what's important to you. I know while I was at the district, I didn't like the culture. I knew I couldn't bring myself to enjoy it as much as I wanted to. I was very interested in the issues and there were great people around me but just the mechanics of the district would drive me crazy! All bureaucracies are frustrating. But I can work with the City bureaucracy.

Alissa: When you're old and gray, looking back on your life, what are the things that you would like to be able to say about your work life?

Samantha: When I reach that point, I would like to look back and say that I had a meaningful career. Not necessarily that I made huge changes in Los Angeles. I think that's a little too much to ask for anyone! The current mayor thinks otherwise, I'm sure. He's out to make changes. If I can feel that I went to work every day, that I did my job, did my best every day, and I enjoyed it, I would be very, very happy. I hear so many people, including people in my family, say, "I go to work every day, and I come home, and that's it." The job is just a job. To me, at this point, I love my job. My job is a really big part of my life. That's the way I look at things and I do things. If I would be able to maintain that type of engagement throughout my career, I would be very happy.

Alissa: Has your work affected the people around you, your community, your circle of friends? Does it affect your social life?

Samantha: I have to think about that. I don't think my friends necessarily know that much about what I do. I mean, they ask, and they listen, and they say, "Hmmm, ok." I'm not sure I'm impacting them personally, but I just try to impart that government employees have a lot of work and that the work we do is actually quite important! Maybe someday I'll break that shell.

Alissa: Suggestions for others who are interested in doing public policy work?

Samantha: Me and my friends, when we were in the masters program, would discuss the pros and cons of working while in the program. It got awfully stressful to be working at times, particularly when I had both jobs. I would say to folks that if they are interested in public policy, they should put themselves into an environment where they can really see whether or not they like it. Had I not worked in the district, I probably would have said, "I would love to be in the district! I would love to see the mechanics and all of that." And I got in there, and as much as I enjoyed the work and I appreciated the partnerships and the relationships that I had, I decided at that point "this is not for me." It's the same with elected officials' offices. At one point, I also decided, "This is not for me. This is just not my cup of tea." People really need to thrive on the fast-paced culture of an elected office. But for me, I look at policy work as a little more bureaucratic, more focused on the long term. Both have been fascinating; both have been interesting. I still get to taste some of that because we do a lot of work for the council offices and the mayor. Ultimately I'm glad that my work focuses on a different type of path—on steady, long-term policy work.

Alissa: Is there anything that I haven't asked you that you want to say?

Samantha: I think some of the top graduate programs in the country are structured in a very technical way, imparting skill sets to use. How do you run a regression? How do you do linear programming? All that type of stuff. I would tell people that you have to be prepared for the politics. I have a friend who currently works in the Comptroller's Office in city hall. The Comptroller's Office used to be just financial auditing. Now, it handles performance evaluation, which is a very different path. The new Comptroller is bringing on a whole lot of new staff. My friend came on board and she said to me, "You know, I don't like the politics of the office. Everything that they do is political." I would have to tell people to be prepared for that. There's nothing that's just pure numbers, just a pure analysis. There is always an intention behind it. As much as we would like to say that you need to be impartial, there's always a direction that is driving whatever analysis you're doing. I think it's more of a critique of the way the programs are structured than anything.

The politics are intangible; I think that's why graduate programs can't focus as much time on them. That's why I think work experience is important. If you don't have that job at the same time you are studying, then your first job is sort of a culture shock to you. You say, "Oh, I have this great skill set, I can do this for you." But we have to listen as policymakers ask, "How much is it going to cost? Are you going to do it in my district?" As a policy analyst, you're not always prepared to do that. As a student you're thinking, "Oh I'm going to weigh the pros and cons. We should only do it in these four districts." Then the other eleven look at you like, "Well, that's not the way it works! If you want eight votes coming out of this meeting, show me why regionally this makes sense." For me, that is probably the thing that was the steepest learning curve. That is always going to be part of the job.

Author Biographies

Alissa S. Wilson was Researcher in Ethics and Human Development at Tufts University and an affiliate at the Global Equity Initiative, Harvard University. As the Practical Idealism Project's resident twenty-something, she traveled the United States interviewing people engaged in social change work. Alissa has served as a Long-term Election Observer with the National Democratic Institute in Nigeria and a Jane Addams–Andrew Carnegie Fellow at the Center on Philanthropy at Indiana University. She has also conducted research at the United Nations and the Carter Center, facilitated peace education trainings in the United States and Nigeria, and worked at arts organizations in New York City. Alissa is an avid dancer and choreographer. She holds a BA from Amherst College in Political Science and a MALD from the Fletcher School of Law and Diplomacy at Tufts University.

Ann Barham is an independent scholar living in Cambridge, Massachusetts. She has been a writer and researcher for a number of commission reports, articles, and books on human development, political activism, and religious engagement. Previously, Ann worked on the personal staff of Senator Susan Collins in Washington, DC, and on distance learning projects at the University of Illinois at Urbana-Champaign. She earned her Bachelors of Foreign Service from Georgetown University and a Masters of Theological Studies from Harvard Divinity School. Ann is currently writing a young adult series that explores the difference between puzzles and true mysteries.

John Hammock is an Associate Professor of Public Policy at the Fletcher School of Law and Diplomacy and at the Friedman School of Nutrition Science and Policy at Tufts University. He is also currently the Managing Director of the Global Equity Initiative at Harvard University and the North American Director of the Oxford Poverty and Human Development Initiative. Dr. Hammock was President of Oxfam America for eleven years and served as Executive Director of ACCION International, which provides credit and technical assistance to micro-enterprises. He holds a doctoral degree in international relations from the Fletcher School at Tufts University and an Honorary Doctor of Laws degree from Denison University. He was born in Cuba. He has two married daughters and two grandchildren.